CRIMINAL JUSTICE, LAW ENFORCEMENT AND CORRECTIONS

JUVENILE JUSTICE

ANNOTATED BIBLIOGRAPHY, LEGISLATIVE HISTORY AND ISSUES

CRIMINAL JUSTICE, LAW ENFORCEMENT AND CORRECTIONS

Additional books in this series can be found on Nova's website under the Series tab.

Additional e-books in this series can be found on Nova's website under the e-book tab.

CRIMINAL JUSTICE, LAW ENFORCEMENT AND CORRECTIONS

JUVENILE JUSTICE

ANNOTATED BIBLIOGRAPHY, LEGISLATIVE HISTORY AND ISSUES

LANA TRAVERSO
EDITOR

nova publishers
New York

For permission to use material from this book please contact us:
Telephone 631-231-7269; Fax 631-231-8175
Web Site: http://www.novapublishers.com

Additional color graphics may be available in the e-book version of this book.

Library of Congress Cataloging-in-Publication Data

ISBN: 978-1-63321-261-9

Published by Nova Science Publishers, Inc. † New York

CONTENTS

Preface		**vii**
Chapter 1	Juvenile Justice: Legislative History and Current Legislative Issues *Kristin M. Finklea*	**1**
Chapter 2	Juvenile Justice Annotated Bibliography *National Institute of Corrections Information Center*	**43**
Index		**145**

PREFACE

Administering justice to juvenile offenders has largely been the domain of the states, and as a result of this the laws that pertain to juvenile offenders can vary widely from state to state. There is no federal juvenile justice system. Although the federal government does not play a direct role in administering juvenile justice, in the 1960s, the federal government began establishing federal juvenile justice agencies and grant programs in order to influence the states' juvenile justice systems. The Juvenile Justice and Delinquency Prevention Act (JJDPA) of 1974 created many of the federal entities and grant programs that continue to operate today, including the Office of Juvenile Justice and Delinquency Prevention (OJJDP) and the State Formula Grants Program. This book analyzes the current federal legislation that influences the state juvenile justice systems. Although the book provides some background information on the evolution of juvenile justice in the United States, the main focus of the book is the major federal legislation that impacts state juvenile justice systems, including the JJDPA. It also provides a bibliography of a comprehensive list of resources about the field of juvenile justice. Each annotation explains what the item is about, and citations are organized into the following areas: courts; juvenile assessment; assessment tools; programs; programs for young women; facilities; training; websites; and juvenile sex offenders.

Chapter 1 – Juvenile justice in the United States has predominantly been the province of the states and their localities. The first juvenile court in America was founded in 1899 in Cook County, Illinois, and, by 1925, all but two states had established juvenile court systems. The mission of these early juvenile courts was to rehabilitate young delinquents instead of just punishing them for their crimes; in practice, this led to marked procedural and substantive differences between the adult and juvenile court systems in the states, including a focus on the offenders and not the offenses, and rehabilitation instead of punishment.

The federal government began to play a role in the states' juvenile justice systems in the 1960s and 1970s. In 1974, Congress passed the first comprehensive piece of juvenile justice legislation, the Juvenile Justice and Delinquency Prevention Act (JJDPA). The JJDPA had three main components: it created a set of institutions within the federal government that were dedicated to coordinating and administering federal juvenile justice efforts; it established grant programs to assist the states with setting up and running their juvenile justice systems; and it promulgated core mandates that states had to adhere to in order to be eligible to receive grant funding. Although the JJDPA has been amended several times over the past 30 years, its basic shape remains similar to that of its original conception.

As it was passed in 1974, the JJDPA focused largely on preventing juvenile delinquency and on rehabilitating juvenile offenders. Subsequent revisions to the act added sanctions and accountability measures to some existing federal grant programs, and new grant programs to the act's purview. In altering the JJDPA to include a greater emphasis on punishing juveniles for their crimes, Congress has essentially followed the lead of the states. During the 1980s and 1990s, most states revised their juvenile justice systems to include more punitive measures and to allow juveniles to be tried as adults in more instances. In 1997, Congress created the Juvenile Accountability Block Grant (JABG), allowing the Attorney General to make grants to states and units of local government to strengthen their juvenile justice systems and foster accountability within their juvenile populations. This has marked a significant change in the philosophy of the juvenile justice system, both at the state level and at the federal level, from its original conception. Juvenile justice in general has thus moved away from emphasizing the rehabilitation of juveniles and toward a greater reliance on sanctioning them for their crimes.

Chapter 2 - This bibliography provides a comprehensive list of resources about the field of juvenile justice. Each annotation explains what the item is about, with many having Web links. Citations are organized into the following areas: courts; juvenile assessment; assessment tools; programs; programs for young women; facilities; training; websites; and juvenile sex offenders.

In: Juvenile Justice
Editor: Lana Traverso

ISBN: 978-1-63321-261-9

Chapter 1

JUVENILE JUSTICE: LEGISLATIVE HISTORY AND CURRENT LEGISLATIVE ISSUES*

Kristin M. Finklea

SUMMARY

Juvenile justice in the United States has predominantly been the province of the states and their localities. The first juvenile court in America was founded in 1899 in Cook County, Illinois, and, by 1925, all but two states had established juvenile court systems. The mission of these early juvenile courts was to rehabilitate young delinquents instead of just punishing them for their crimes; in practice, this led to marked procedural and substantive differences between the adult and juvenile court systems in the states, including a focus on the offenders and not the offenses, and rehabilitation instead of punishment.

The federal government began to play a role in the states' juvenile justice systems in the 1960s and 1970s. In 1974, Congress passed the first comprehensive piece of juvenile justice legislation, the Juvenile Justice and Delinquency Prevention Act (JJDPA). The JJDPA had three main components: it created a set of institutions within the federal government that were dedicated to coordinating and administering federal juvenile justice efforts; it established grant programs to assist the states with setting up and running their juvenile justice systems; and it promulgated core mandates that

* This is an edited, reformatted and augmented version of a Congressional Research Service publication, No. RL33947, dated November 27, 2012.

states had to adhere to in order to be eligible to receive grant funding. Although the JJDPA has been amended several times over the past 30 years, its basic shape remains similar to that of its original conception.

As it was passed in 1974, the JJDPA focused largely on preventing juvenile delinquency and on rehabilitating juvenile offenders. Subsequent revisions to the act added sanctions and accountability measures to some existing federal grant programs, and new grant programs to the act's purview. In altering the JJDPA to include a greater emphasis on punishing juveniles for their crimes, Congress has essentially followed the lead of the states. During the 1980s and 1990s, most states revised their juvenile justice systems to include more punitive measures and to allow juveniles to be tried as adults in more instances. In 1997, Congress created the Juvenile Accountability Block Grant (JABG), allowing the Attorney General to make grants to states and units of local government to strengthen their juvenile justice systems and foster accountability within their juvenile populations. This has marked a significant change in the philosophy of the juvenile justice system, both at the state level and at the federal level, from its original conception. Juvenile justice in general has thus moved away from emphasizing the rehabilitation of juveniles and toward a greater reliance on sanctioning them for their crimes.

Authorization for the JJDPA's main provisions expired at the end of FY2007 and FY2008, but its major programs have continued to receive appropriations. Congress may choose to consider the JJDPA's reauthorization. Policy issues associated with its reauthorization include what the best federal response to juvenile violence and juvenile crime should be; whether the system should focus on the rehabilitation of juvenile offenders or on holding juvenile offenders accountable for their actions; and whether the grant programs as currently comprised represent the best way to support juvenile justice efforts in the states. Similarly, authorization for the JABG expired at the end of FY2009. One of the issues surrounding its potential reauthorization involves whether grant program purpose areas should be modified, expanded, or clarified.

INTRODUCTION

Administering justice to juvenile offenders has largely been the domain of the states, and as a result of this the laws that pertain to juvenile offenders can vary widely from state to state. There is no federal juvenile justice system. Although the federal government does not play a direct role in administering juvenile justice, in the 1960s, the federal government began establishing federal juvenile justice agencies and grant programs in order to influence the states' juvenile justice systems. The Juvenile Justice and Delinquency Prevention Act (JJDPA) of 1974 created many of the federal entities and grant programs that continue to operate today, including the Office of Juvenile Justice and Delinquency Prevention (OJJDP) and the State Formula Grants Program. Eligibility for many of these grant programs is tied to certain mandates that the states must adhere to in order to receive federal funding. Over the ensuing decades, the JJDPA has been modified a number of times, broadening the mandate of the agencies it created and adding to the grant programs it established.

This report analyzes the current federal legislation that influences the state juvenile justice systems. Although the report provides some background information on the evolution of juvenile justice in the United States, the main focus of the report is the major federal legislation that impacts state juvenile justice systems, including the JJDPA. As the major provisions of the JJDPA expired in FY2007 and FY2008, several issues pertaining to its reauthorization may be of concern to Congress, including, but not limited to, the following:

- Should the core mandates associated with the state formula grants be expanded or modified?
- Are the current grant programs effective?
- Is there sufficient coordination occurring at the federal level?
- Should the federal approach to juvenile justice focus on rehabilitation, accountability, or both philosophies?

The original JJDPA and its major revisions through the end of the 109th Congress are addressed in **Appendix A** and **Appendix B**.

BACKGROUND

Juvenile justice in the United States has been predominantly the province of the states and their localities. The first juvenile court in America was founded in 1899 in Cook County, Illinois. Twenty-five years later, all but two states had enacted legislation establishing a separate juvenile court system for young offenders. The mission of these juvenile courts was to attempt to turn young delinquents into productive adults rather than merely punishing them for their crimes. This led to marked procedural and substantive differences between the adult and juvenile court systems in the states, including a focus on the offenders and not the offenses, and on rehabilitation instead of punishment.[1]

The federal government began to play a role in the states' juvenile justice systems in the 1960s and 1970s. In the Juvenile Delinquency and Youth Offenses Control Act,[2] Congress provided funds for state and local governments, through the Department of Health, Education, and Welfare, to conduct demonstration projects to research improved methods for preventing and controlling crime committed by juveniles. In 1968, Congress passed additional legislation[3] to provide direct assistance to state and local governments and to train juvenile justice personnel. To receive funding, states were required to designate a single agency to take the lead in improving delinquency prevention and control programs. Also in 1968, Congress for the first time placed juvenile justice grant authority within the purview of the Department of Justice (DOJ).

Despite these congressional efforts to provide assistance to the states as they attempted to rein in juvenile crime, juvenile arrests for violent crimes increased by 216% between 1960 and 1974.[4] This increase in juvenile violent crime outstripped the growth in the juvenile population; the under-18 population grew from 47 million in 1950 to 70 million in 1970—an increase of only 49%.[5] It seemed apparent that the technical assistance and financial aid that Congress had provided the states was not enough to address the growing problem of juvenile crime, and many commentators maintained that there was a need for a distinct federal entity to manage the federal government's response to juvenile delinquency. In 1974, Congress addressed the issue by passing the first comprehensive piece of juvenile justice legislation, the JJDPA.[6] The JJDPA created a number of grant programs and established a new federal agency within DOJ—OJJDP—to oversee these grant programs and to coordinate the federal government-wide response to juvenile delinquency.

In the 1980s, many states responded to the public perception that juvenile crime was increasing by passing more punitive laws for juvenile offenders. Some of these laws removed certain types of juvenile crimes from the juvenile court system altogether, mandating that they be handled by the adult criminal system instead. Other laws instituted mandatory sentences for juvenile offenders convicted of certain crimes. This movement toward punishing juveniles and away from working to rehabilitate them accelerated in the 1990s, with all but three states passing laws that modified or removed traditional juvenile court confidentiality agreements, all but five states passing laws easing the transfer of juveniles into the adult criminal justice system, and a majority of states passing laws expanding sentencing options for juveniles.[7] During this period, more punitive measures were incorporated into the accepted federal funding streams for juvenile justice programs through a series of revisions to the JJDPA. These revisions are described in **Appendix A** and **Appendix B**.

JUVENILE JUSTICE HISTORY

The First Juvenile Courts

The early criminal justice system in America did not include a separate juvenile justice system. The colonists brought the British criminal justice system with them to the new world. This system included forced apprenticeship for poor and neglected children. If a juvenile committed a crime, they were first warned, shamed, or given corporeal punishment and then returned to the community. If a child committed a major criminal act, however, they were treated and tried as adults. Trials and punishment were largely based on the offender's age; anybody over the age of seven was subject to a trial in criminal court.[8] These early American laws had three fundamental features: establishing local control of the justice system, giving families the responsibility (and legal liability) for their children's actions, and distinguishing between deserving and undeserving poor people.[9]

The first juvenile court in the United States was established in Chicago in 1899. By 1925, all but two states had established separate juvenile justice systems.[10] The Juvenile Court of Chicago was based on the British doctrine of *parens patriae*, or the notion of the state acting in the nature of a parent. This doctrine was used to explain the state's interest in distinguishing between adults and children in its dispensation of justice. Because children are not fully imbued with developmental or legal capacity, the *parens patriae* doctrine held that the government could provide protection and treatment for children whose parents were not providing adequate care or supervision.[11] The Juvenile Court of Chicago became the model for the various state juvenile justice systems that followed it. Its key features were the definition of a juvenile as a child under the age of 16; the separation of children and adults in correctional institutions; the establishment of special, informal procedural rules, including the elimination of indictments, pleadings, and jury trials; the provision of probation officers to monitor juveniles released into the community; and the prohibition of the detention of children below the age of 12 in a jail or police station.[12]

Although delinquency among children was punished, key elements of the juvenile justice system as it was originally conceived were the welfare of the child and the concept that delinquent children could be transformed into productive citizens through treatment. This benevolent mission was clearly stated in most laws that established juvenile justice systems, and led to substantial procedural and substantive differences between juvenile and adult criminal justice systems in the states. For example, juvenile court intake considered extra-legal factors—such as the child's home situation—as well as legal factors when deciding whether to bring a case to trial, and had the discretion to handle cases informally.[13]

Additionally, these early juvenile courts did not incorporate the procedural due process protections afforded adult criminal defendants, which were deemed unnecessary as a result of the court's benevolent mission. Attorneys for the state and the youth being tried were not considered essential to the system's operation, especially in less serious cases, and judges had a broad range of dispositions at their disposal that were tailored to the best interests of the child. Judges' dispositions became part of a treatment plan for the juvenile, and this treatment continued until the juvenile was considered cured or became an adult at age 21.[14]

In 1914, the practice of *diversion*, or the official halting of formal criminal proceedings against a juvenile offender, was established with the creation of the Chicago Boy's Court. The goal of diversion was to provide treatment for juveniles outside of the formal juvenile justice system. To this end, the juvenile court in Chicago released juveniles to the supervision and authority of various community service agencies, who evaluated the youth's behavior and reported back to the Court. If the evaluation was satisfactory to the judge, the court officially discharged the juvenile without any formal record of the proceedings.[15]

By 1930, only the federal government continued to treat children who were charged with a crime as adults.[16] This situation led the U.S. Attorney General to recommend that juveniles charged with violating federal laws be returned to their home state's juvenile justice system, a proposition that Congress agreed with.[17]

Early Federal Government Efforts

The earliest federal government involvement in juvenile delinquency occurred in 1909, when the White House held a Conference on the Care of Dependent Children. The goal of this conference was to share information about needy children across the United States and to emphasize the immediate need for action. This conference led directly to the creation of the U.S. Children's Bureau in 1912. The Children's Bureau was authorized to investigate and report on all aspects of child welfare, including the juvenile justice system.[18] In 1936, the Children's Bureau began providing the first federal subsidy program that provided child welfare grants to states. These grants were used to care for a wide array of at-risk youth, including juvenile delinquents.

The first major federal legislation addressing juvenile delinquents was enacted in 1938. The Federal Juvenile Delinquency Act of 1938 (FJDA)[19] left the state juvenile justice systems as the preferred alternative for juveniles arrested for violating federal laws, but gave the Attorney General the discretion to charge a juvenile as an adult and allowed for federal juvenile proceedings if both parties agreed to it.

In 1951, Congress amended the FJDA with the Federal Youth Corrections Act.[20] This act afforded juvenile offenders tried as adults in the federal system special rehabilitation outcomes. Apart from this revision, however, the FJDA remained essentially unchanged for 35 years until Congress passed major Juvenile Justice reform measures in the 1970s. In 1951, Congress also established the Juvenile Delinquency Bureau within the Department of Health, Education, and Welfare (HEW). The bureau's placement within HEW can be seen as a reflection of the early governmental focus on the treatment of juvenile delinquents and the prevention of delinquency, rather than on punishment.[21]

In the 1950s and 1960s, however, many observers began to question the juvenile courts' ability to successfully rehabilitate delinquents. While the system's basic goal of rehabilitating juveniles through individually tailored plans was not in question, professionals in the field grew concerned about the growing numbers of juveniles being institutionalized for treatment purposes. This concern was reflected in a series of Supreme Court rulings during the 1960s that required that juvenile court procedures become more formal in order to afford juveniles legal protections comparable to those afforded adults in criminal courts.[22]

The landmark Supreme Court ruling of this period, *In re Gault*,[23] concluded that hearings that could result in the institutionalization of children must afford the juveniles being tried the right to notice and counsel, the right to question witnesses, and the right to protection from self-incrimination. Although the Court did not include the right to appellate review in its decision, it encouraged the states to afford juveniles that protection as well.[24]

Congress responded to the increasing public awareness of juvenile crime by passing the Juvenile Delinquency and Youth Offenses Control Act of 1961.[25] This act authorized HEW to provide grants totaling $10 million annually, for three years, to states, local government entities, and private nonprofit agencies to fund demonstration projects that focused on improving the methods used to prevent and control juvenile crime. The projects funded through this initiative were focused on urban inner-cities that had the highest juvenile delinquency rates at the time.[26]

In 1968, Congress took two further actions that affected federal funding for juvenile justice. The first was the Juvenile Delinquency Prevention and Control Act,[27] which provided grant funding to the states and local government entities for the training of juvenile court personnel. These grants were to be administered by HEW. The second was the Omnibus Crime Control and Safe Streets Act,[28] which, among other things, involved DOJ in juvenile justice for the first time through the Law Enforcement Assistance Administration (LEAA), which was created in Title I of the act. LEAA was to serve as a clearinghouse for channeling federal funding to state and local law enforcement agencies, giving states incentives to establish planning agencies, and funding a wide variety of programs ranging from education and research to local crime control initiatives.[29]

By the early 1970s, consensus began to form around the idea that the federal government's efforts to address juvenile justice were unfocused and underfunded.[30] The House Committee on Education and Labor in particular questioned the effectiveness of the Juvenile Delinquency Prevention and Control Act of 1968 and levied a number of criticisms at the way HEW implemented the act:

> The HEW administered program, during its first three years, was disappointing because of delay and inefficiency. A director of the Youth Development and Delinquency Prevention Administration was not appointed for over 18 months. Less than a third of the $150 million authorized for fiscal years 1968 through 1971 was appropriated. Furthermore, only half of the funds that were appropriated were actually expended. The funds were generally spent

on underfunded, unrelated, and scattered projects. Weakness in program administration, the dominance of the Law Enforcement Assistance Administration, and inadequate funding contributed to reasons for a lack of total success.[31]

Disappointed with the way the 1968 Act was implemented, consensus began to form within Congress around the idea of creating a new federal entity to oversee the federal government's juvenile justice efforts. As the Juvenile Delinquency Prevention and Control Act's authorization was expiring in 1974, Congress moved to replace it with a more comprehensive piece of legislation.

THE JUVENILE JUSTICE AND DELINQUENCY PREVENTION ACT (JJDPA)

The JJDPA was first passed by Congress in 1974[32] and was most recently reauthorized in 2002 by the 21st Century Department of Justice Appropriations Authorization Act.[33] Authorization for its main provisions expired in FY2007 and FY2008. This section analyzes the JJDPA as it stands today.

By 1974, strong momentum had developed in the public, academic, and governmental arenas toward the idea that the juvenile justice system needed to focus on preventing juvenile delinquency, deinstitutionalizing youth already in the system, and keeping juvenile offenders separate from adult offenders. Congress responded to this growing consensus by passing the Juvenile Justice and Delinquency Prevention Act of 1974. The JJDPA had three main components:

- it created a set of institutions within the federal government that were dedicated to coordinating and administering federal juvenile justice efforts;
- it established grant programs to assist the states with setting up and running their juvenile justice systems; and
- it promulgated core mandates that states had to adhere to in order to be eligible to receive grant funding.

Although the JJDPA has been amended several times over the past 30 years, it continues to feature the same three components. As it was passed in 1974, the JJDPA focused the federal government's efforts largely on preventing juvenile delinquency and on rehabilitating juvenile offenders.

Subsequent revisions to the act placed emphasis on influencing states to expand the use of sanctions and accountability measures through some existing grant programs, as well as adding new grant programs to the act's purview. The latest reauthorization of the JJDPA, enacted by P.L. 107-273, made several changes to the act, including consolidating various separate grant programs and modifying the language of some of the core mandates. **Appendix A** details the original JJDPA; **Appendix B** details the JJDPA's major subsequent revisions and includes a summary of the specific changes enacted by its last reauthorization.

Concentration of Federal Efforts

The original JJDPA established OJJDP within DOJ's Law Enforcement Assistance Administration[34] (LEAA) as the new clearinghouse for the federal government's efforts to influence states' juvenile justice systems. Subsequent revisions to the JJPDA designated OJJDP as a stand-alone office within DOJ and directed the Administrator to report directly to the Attorney General. Today, the JJDPA grants the Administrator of OJJDP a broad authority to coordinate the federal government's activities relating to the treatment of juvenile offenders, including programs that focus on prevention, diversion, training, treatment, rehabilitation, evaluation, research, and improvement of the states' juvenile justice systems.[35] The Administrator is charged with developing objectives, priorities, strategies, and long-term plans concerning the treatment and handling of juvenile offenders by federal agencies and by the states, and overseeing the implementation of these plans. Thus, the Administrator of OJJDP is, by statute, the lead individual in the U.S. federal government charged with developing and implementing policies that govern the treatment of juvenile offenders by federal agencies and the federal government's efforts to influence the states' juvenile justice systems.

Coordinating Council on Juvenile Justice and Delinquency Prevention

The original JJDPA established an independent organization known as the Coordinating Council on Juvenile Justice and Delinquency Prevention (Coordinating Council) to coordinate the federal government's juvenile delinquency programs. The Coordinating Council was to be composed of representatives from a broad range of federal agencies who "exercise significant decision making authority in the Federal agency involved."[36]

Subsequent revisions to the JJDPA expanded the number of agencies represented on the Coordinating Council.

Today, the Coordinating Council is an independent organization within the federal government charged with coordinating all federal juvenile delinquency programs, all federal programs that deal with unaccompanied minors, and all federal programs relating to missing and exploited children.[37] The Coordinating Council is composed of the heads of all the federal agencies that touch on these broad areas, including the Attorney General, the Secretary of Health and Human Services, the Secretary of Labor, the Secretary of Education, the Secretary of Housing and Urban Development, the Administrator of OJJDP, the Director of the Office of National Drug Control Policy, the Chief Executive Officer of the Corporation for National and Community Service, and the Commissioner of Immigration and Naturalization (now the Commissioner of U.S. Immigration and Customs Enforcement). In addition to these standing members, the Coordinating Council is composed of nine other members, of which three are appointed by the President, three are appointed by the Speaker of the House, and three are appointed by the majority leader of the Senate. These nine members are to be juvenile justice practitioners who are not officers or employees of the U.S. government, and they are to serve one- to three-year terms. The Attorney General acts as the Chairman of the Council, and the Administrator of OJJDP serves as the Vice Chairman of the Council.

In essence, the role of the Coordinating Council is to coordinate the overall federal government policy and development of objectives and priorities for federal programs dealing with juvenile delinquency and unaccompanied minors. As a function of this, the Coordinating Council is charged with examining how the various programs in the federal government are operating and to report to Congress on the degree to which federal agency funds are being used for purposes consistent with the core mandates required in the state plans.[38] The Council is also charged with reviewing why federal agencies take juveniles into custody and to make recommendations for how to improve the federal government's practices and facilities for detaining juveniles.

Annual Report

Starting in 1988, Congress required OJJDP to produce an annual report to Congress on the agency's operations. This report, by statute, must summarize and analyze the most recent data available to the federal government concerning the detention of juveniles, describe the activities funded by OJJDP and the activities of the Coordinating Council, identify the extent to which each state complies with the core mandates and their state plan requirements, and evaluate the effectiveness of federal juvenile delinquency programs in reducing the incidences of delinquency and violent crime among juveniles.[39]

State Formula Grants

The original JJDPA authorized OJJDP to make formula grants[40] to states, which can be used to fund the planning, establishment, operation, coordination, and evaluation of projects for the development of more effective juvenile delinquency programs and improved juvenile justice systems. Although this grant program has been modified through the intervening years, it remains in place today as one of the core components of the federal approach to influencing states' juvenile justice systems. Authorization for this program expired in FY2007, but it has continued to receive appropriations.

Funds are allocated annually among the states on the basis of relative proportion of the population under the age of 18. However, the JJDPA sets minimum amounts that can be provided to the states depending on the total appropriation for the State Formula Grants Program, which are outlined in **Table 1**. No more than 10% of the state's allocation can be used for administrative expenses, including creating the state juvenile justice plans and disbursing the grant funds. Additionally, funds used for administrative expenses must be matched by state or local funds. The JJDPA authorizes "such sums as may be necessary" through FY2007 to carry out the State Formula Grants Program.[41]

Table 1. Minimum Formula Grant Amounts

Total Appropriation	State Minimums	Territorya Minimums
Less than $75,000,000	$325,000 to $400,000	$75,000 to $100,000
$75,000,000 and above	$600,000	$100,000

Source: 42 U.S.C. §5631.

Note: For any state to receive funding above the minimums, the allocation for every state or territory must exceed the appropriation they received in 2000.

a. Territory refers to the Virgin Islands of the United States, Guam, American Samoa, and the Commonwealth of the Northern Mariana Islands.

JJDPA Formula Grant Mandates[42]

To receive formula grant funding through the JJDPA, states are required to formulate plans for the administration of juvenile justice within their jurisdiction and to submit yearly reports to OJJDP concerning their progress in implementing the programs being funded. The JJDPA stipulates a list of components that must be included in state plans, funding constraints for how the state formula grants can be apportioned, and four core mandates that must be adhered to in order to receive funding.

State Plan Components

To receive state formula grant funding, states must submit a juvenile justice plan to OJJDP. Should the state fail to do so, or if the Administrator determines that the state's plan does not meet the requirements elucidated in 42 U.S.C. §5633 (a), OJJDP can make the formula grant funding available to local public and private nonprofit agencies within the state for use in activities that help the state meet the four core mandates. The following plan components are required of all states receiving funding:

- States must designate an agency to supervise the administration of the juvenile justice plan and show that this agency has the legal authority to implement the plan. States must also consult with local government entities as they formulate the plan.
- States must provide for an advisory group of 15 to 33 members that participate in the development and review of the state's juvenile justice plan.[43]
- States must provide for the analysis of juvenile delinquency issues within their jurisdiction, including a description of the services provided to address the issues and performance goals and priorities for the implementation of these services. States are also directed to formulate a plan for providing gender-specific services, a plan for providing juvenile justice services in rural areas, and a plan for providing needed mental health services to juveniles.

Formula Grant Allocation

The JJDPA places several restrictions on how the funding received through the state formula grant program can be allocated within the states and territories. At least two-thirds of the funds received through the formula grant program must be passed through to units of local government, including Indian tribes[44] and local private agencies. Private agencies must have first applied to a local unit of government for funding and been turned down before being eligible for formula grant funding, and all expenditures must be consistent with the state's plan. Funding must be distributed equitably throughout the state, including rural areas.

Additionally, at least 75% of the funds provided to the state must be used for a wide array of juvenile justice related programs, including, but not limited to

- community based alternatives to incarceration;
- counseling, mentoring, and training programs within the juvenile justice system as well as similar community based programs and services, including aftercare and after-school programs;
- comprehensive juvenile justice and delinquency prevention programs that assist the coordination of service provision among the various players involved;
- providing services to address child abuse and neglect;
- expanding the use of probation offices;
- programs that address the relationship between juvenile delinquency and learning disabilities, and programs that help juveniles and their families overcome language barriers;
- projects designed to deter juvenile gang members from participating in illegal activities, including those that promote their involvement in lawful activities;
- substance and drug abuse prevention and treatment programs, including mental health programs;
- programs that focus on positive youth development for at-risk youth and juvenile offenders;
- programs that focus on strengthening families and providing them assistance to ensure juveniles have a nurturing home environment;
- programs that provide mental health services to juveniles at every stage of the juvenile justice process; and
- programs that encourage juvenile courts to develop a continuum of post-adjudication restraints that bridge the gap between probation and detention in a juvenile correctional facility.[45]

Core Mandates

The original JJDPA included two core requirements, or mandates, that states had to adhere to in order to receive formula grant funding. Subsequent revisions to the JJDPA expanded the list of core mandates to the four that exist today. Failure to adhere to these requirements will result in a 20% reduction of funding for each of the four mandates with which the state is not in compliance. Additionally, the state will be ineligible for future funding unless: the state agrees to spend 50% of the allocated funding to achieving compliance with whichever mandate it is noncompliant with; the Administrator of OJJDP determines that the state has achieved "substantial compliance"; or the state has demonstrated an "unequivocal commitment to achieving full compliance with such applicable requirements within a reasonable time."[46] Following are the four core mandates as they are codified today:

- Deinstitutionalization of status offences (DSO). Juveniles who are charged with or who have committed an offense that would not be a crime if committed by an adult, and juveniles who are not charged with any offenses, are not to be placed in secure detention or secure correctional facilities.[47]
- Juveniles are not to be detained or confined in any institution in which they would have contact with adult inmates. Additionally, correctional staff that work with both adult and juvenile offenders must have been trained and certified to work with juveniles.
- Juveniles are not to be detained or confined in any jail or lockup for adults, except for juveniles who are accused of non-status offenses. These juveniles may be detained for no longer than six hours as they are processed, waiting to be released, awaiting transfer to a juvenile facility, or awaiting their court appearance. Additionally, juveniles in rural locations may be held for up to 48 hours in jails or lockups for adults as they await their initial court appearance. Juveniles held in adult jails or lockups in both rural and urban areas are not to have contact with adult inmates, and any staff working with both adults and juveniles must have been trained and certified to work with juveniles.
- Disproportionate minority contact (DMC). States are required to show that they are implementing juvenile delinquency prevention programs designed to reduce—without establishing or requiring numerical standards or quotas—the disproportionate number of minorities confined within their juvenile justice systems.

Juvenile Delinquency Prevention Block Grants

In addition to the formula grants, the JJDPA also authorizes OJJDP to make grants available to carry out projects designed to prevent juvenile delinquency.[48] The 21st Century Department of Justice Appropriations Authorization Act[49] folded several pre-existing grant programs into the Juvenile Delinquency Prevention Block Grant program and authorized "such sums as may be necessary" for this purpose through FY2007.[50] As a result of this consolidation, purpose areas that may be funded through the block grant program comprise a wide array of services, treatments, and interventions, including, but not limited to the following:[51]

- Projects that provide treatment to juvenile offenders and at risk juveniles who are victims of child abuse or neglect, or who have experienced violence at home, at school, or in their communities. Additionally, the program can fund projects providing treatment and services to the families of these juveniles.
- Educational projects or support services for juveniles that focus on encouraging juveniles to stay in school; aiding in the transition from school to work; helping identify juveniles who have learning difficulties and disabilities both in school and in the juvenile justice system; encouraging new approaches to preventing school violence and vandalism; developing locally coordinated policies among education, juvenile justice, and social service agencies; and providing mental health services.
- Projects that expand the use of probation officers, especially for programs that permit nonviolent juvenile offenders to remain at home instead of being placed in an institution, and to ensure that juveniles complete the terms of their probation.
- Counseling, training, and mentoring programs, particularly for juveniles residing in low-income and high-crime areas.
- Community based projects and services aimed at reducing juvenile delinquency, including literacy and social service programs.
- Drug and alcohol abuse treatment programs.
- Postsecondary education and training scholarship programs for low income juveniles residing in neighborhoods with high rates of poverty, violence, and drug related crimes.
- Projects that establish an initial intake screening and evaluation of juveniles taken into custody, both to determine the likelihood that the

juvenile will commit crimes in the future and to provide the appropriate interventions to prevent future crimes.

- Projects designed to prevent juveniles from participating in organized criminal gangs.

Grant funding is allocated to the eligible states based on the proportion of their population that is under the age of 18. To become eligible for these grants, states must submit an application assuring that no more than 5% of the grant will be used for administrative, evaluation, and technical assistance costs and that federal grant funding will supplement, and not supplant, state and local juvenile delinquency prevention efforts. Additionally, the state must have submitted a plan. This grant program has not received appropriations to date; rather the annual appropriation for OJJDP continues to follow the previous structure, and funds have been appropriated in each subsequent fiscal year for some of the grant programs that were repealed in 2002. The authorization for this program expired in FY2007.

Part E: Developing, Testing, and Demonstrating Promising New Initiatives and Programs (Challenge Grants)

The Challenge Grants program[52] was originally added in 1992 and was modified by the 21st Century Department of Justice Appropriations Authorization Act, which authorized "such sums as may be necessary" to carry out the program through FY2007. It replaced the Demonstration Programs grant that had been created by the original JJDPA (see Appendix A and Appendix B for more information on the prior grant programs). The Challenge Grants program authorizes OJJDP to make discretionary grants to state, local, and tribal governments and private entities to carry out programs that will develop, test, or demonstrate promising new initiatives that may prevent, control, or reduce juvenile delinquency. The Administrator is charged with ensuring that these grants are apportioned in such a way as to ensure an equitable geographical distribution of these projects throughout the United States. The program is currently unauthorized, and it last received appropriations in FY2010.

Title V Incentive Grants for Local Delinquency Prevention Programs

The Incentive Grants for Local Delinquency Prevention program[53] authorizes OJJDP to make discretionary grants to the states that are then transmitted to units of local government in order to carry out delinquency prevention programs for juveniles who have come into contact with, or are likely to come into contact with, the juvenile justice system. Unlike the other grant programs within the JJDPA, which are authorized through FY2007, the 21st Century Department of Justice Reauthorization Act authorized "such sums as may be necessary" for the Title V grant program through FY2008. The program is currently unauthorized, but has continued to receive appropriations.

Activities that can be funded through the Title V Incentive Grants for Local Delinquency Prevention program include the following:

- alcohol and substance abuse prevention services;
- educational programs;
- child and adolescent health (as well as mental health) services;
- recreational programs;
- leadership programs;
- programs that teach juveniles that they are accountable for their actions;
- job or skills training programs; and
- other "data-driven evidence based prevention programs."

As it reviews the grant applications that it receives, OJJDP is to give priority to programs that

- include plans for service and agency coordination (including co-location of services);
- coordinate and collaborate with the Delinquency Prevention Block Grant recipients in the state;
- include innovative ways to involve the private sector in delinquency prevention activities;
- help states develop or enhance state-wide subsidy programs for early intervention and prevention of juvenile delinquency; and
- develop data-driven prevention plans and utilize evidence-based prevention strategies (including conducting program evaluations to

determine the impact and effectiveness of the programs being funded).

Local government entities are eligible for funding if they are in compliance with the state plan requirements, and if they have submitted to the state's advisory group a three-year comprehensive plan outlining their plans for investing in delinquency prevention activities and for coordinating services delivered to at-risk juveniles and their families. Funding to local government entities is disbursed by the state, and these grants are conditioned on a 50% match by either the local entity or the state.

Thus, the JJDPA includes four major grant programs within its purview: the State Formula Grant program, the Delinquency Prevention Block Grant program, the Challenge Grant program, and the Title V Incentive Grants for Local Delinquency Prevention program. The first three grant programs, located within Title II of the act, were authorized through FY2007. The Title V grant program was authorized through FY2008. While these grant programs differ slightly, they each provide funding for a wide array of juvenile delinquency prevention purposes. The State Formula Grant program and the Delinquency Prevention Block Grant program feature long lists of detailed purpose areas that overlap. Conversely, the Challenge Grant and the Title V grant programs feature broadly written purpose areas that provide more discretion to OJJDP in their administration. Although this report does not include appropriations data, it is important to note that the appropriators have not funded the Delinquency Prevention Block Grant since its inception. Instead, the appropriators have continued to fund some of the grant programs repealed in 2002 either as stand-alone appropriations or as carve-outs within the Title V grant program. This issue will be discussed in greater detail in the "Issues for Congress" section of this report.

JUVENILE ACCOUNTABILITY BLOCK GRANTS

The Juvenile Accountability Block Grant (JABG) program was originally created by the FY1998 DOJ Appropriations Act (P.L. 105-119) and was appropriated each subsequent fiscal year. However, the JABG program was codified by the 21st Century Department of Justice Reauthorization Act (P.L. 107-273) in Subtitle A of Title II of the act.[54] As such it falls outside the scope of the JJDPA, but nevertheless comprises a significant component of the federal government's approach to juvenile justice.

The JABG program authorizes the Attorney General to make grants to states[55] and units of local government to strengthen their juvenile justice systems and foster accountability within their juvenile populations. The program focuses resources on holding juveniles accountable for their actions and building up the juvenile justice system in the states. It also essentially signifies the high-water mark of the federal government's movement away from an emphasis on rehabilitating juveniles and toward the idea that juveniles need to be punished for their crimes; indeed, the only core mandate of the JABG program is that states must begin to implement a system of graduated sanctions[56] in order to be eligible for funding.

As originally codified, the JABG program authorized funding for 16 accountability-based purpose areas, including, but not limited to, implementing graduated sanctions; building or operating juvenile correction or detention facilities; hiring juvenile court officers, including judges, probation officers, and special advocates; and hiring additional juvenile prosecutors. The act also authorized a separate Tribal Grant program within the JABG appropriation to fund accountability-based measures aimed at strengthening the tribal juvenile justice systems. The JABG program was last authorized in 2006 by P.L. 109-162, which added a purpose area to the original 16 areas and authorized JABG at $350 million a year through FY2009. The program is currently unauthorized, but has continued to receive appropriations.

Purpose Areas

As currently comprised, the program authorizes funding for 17 accountability based purpose areas, including, but not limited to

- implementing graduated sanctions;
- building or operating juvenile correction or detention facilities;
- hiring and training juvenile court officers, including judges, probation officers, special advocates, juvenile prosecutors, and detention or corrections personnel;
- supporting prosecutorial initiatives aimed at curbing drug use, violence, and gangs;
- establishing juvenile drug courts and gun courts;
- establishing juvenile records and information sharing systems between the courts, schools, and social service agencies to keep better track of repeat offenders;

- using risk and needs assessments to facilitate effective early interventions for mental health and substance abuse issues;
- accountability-based school safety initiatives;
- establishing and improving pre-release and post-release programs to help juveniles reintegrate into the community; and
- restorative justice programs that emphasize the moral accountability of an offender toward their victims and the affected community.

Eligibility Requirements

The JABG program awards grants to the states; most of this funding is then sub-granted to units of local government. States and local entities must provide information about the activities that will be carried out with the grant funding and the criteria that will be used to assess whether the programs were effective (including the extent to which evidence-based practices were utilized). Additionally, states and local governments must provide assurances that the they are working toward implementing laws effecting the use of graduated sanctions for juvenile offenders.

As mentioned, the implementation of graduated sanctions is the only core mandate associated with the JABG program. These graduated sanctions should, at a minimum, ensure that

- sanctions are imposed on juvenile offenders for each delinquent offense they commit;
- sanctions escalate in intensity with each subsequent more serious offense;
- there is enough flexibility to tailor sanctions and services to each individual juvenile offender; and
- appropriate consideration is given when handing out sanctions to the victims of the crime and public safety in general.

States are allowed to participate in the program if their graduated sanctions are discretionary rather than mandatory, but must require each juvenile court in its jurisdiction to submit an annual report concerning the extent to which graduated sanctions were implemented and the reasons for which graduated sanctions were not applied. This information should be collected by units of local government and reported to the states, which in turn report it to the Attorney General. Eligible states and units of local government are also required to establish and convene an advisory board that is charged with recommending a coordinated enforcement plan for the use of the JABG funds awarded. The board is to include, where appropriate, members of the state or local police, the prosecutors office, the juvenile court, the probation office, the education system, the social service system, a nonprofit victim advocacy organization, and a nonprofit religious or community group.

JABG Allocation

Of the total amount appropriated for the JABG program, each state is automatically allocated 0.5%. The remaining 75% of the JABG funding is then allocated to the states in accordance to the ratio of their population of juveniles under the age of 18 to the overall population of juveniles under the age of 18 in the United States that fiscal year. The states must pass along not less than 75% of the funds they receive to units of local government, unless the state can demonstrably certify that their overall juvenile justice costs are more than 25% of the aggregate amount of juvenile justice expenditures in the state (i.e., the states expenditures plus all the units of local government expenditures) that fiscal year and that they have consulted with as many units of local government as practicable regarding their expenditures. States are required to pass along the funding to units of local government according to a formula that is based on the ratio of the local government's juvenile justice costs and the juvenile violent crimes[57] committed in their jurisdiction to the overall juvenile justice costs and juvenile violent crimes in the state.

The Attorney General is authorized to make grants directly to specially qualified units of local government if the states do not qualify or apply for JABG funding. In these cases, the Attorney General is authorized to reserve up to 75% of that states allocation to make grants directly to units of local government that meet the funding requirements outlined above. Lastly, the Attorney General is authorized to use the average amount allocated by the states to their units of local governments as the basis for the amounts awarded to these specially qualified units of local government.

Of the total amount awarded to a state or a unit of local government, only 5% can be used to pay for administrative costs. Funds awarded under JABG cannot be used to supplant existing funding but must instead be used to increase the amount of funding that would otherwise be available to the state juvenile justice systems. The federal share of the activities funded through a JABG grant cannot exceed 90%, except for JABG funds used to construct juvenile court or detention facilities in which case the federal share is not to exceed 50%.

ISSUES FOR CONGRESS

Congress may choose to consider the JJDPA's reauthorization because its major provisions expired at the end of FY2007 and FY2008. Similarly, the JABG expired at the end of FY2009, and Congress may also consider its reauthorization. As Congress debates reauthorizing funding for juvenile justice programs, it faces the same issues that have revolved around the juvenile justice system for more than 30 years:

- What is the appropriate federal role in an arena that has predominantly been the province of the states?
- What is the appropriate federal response to juvenile violence and juvenile crime?
- Should federal efforts to influence the states' juvenile justice systems focus on the rehabilitation of juvenile offenders, on holding juvenile offenders accountable for their actions, or some combination of both?
- Are the grant programs as currently comprised the best way to support juvenile justice efforts in the states?

The following section provides a more detailed examination of these potential issues.

Rehabilitation Versus Accountability

As previously noted, the fundamental tension within the juvenile justice system over the past 30 years has been the relationship between rehabilitating juveniles and holding them accountable for their actions. To some extent, this is an arbitrary distinction in that the system as currently comprised includes both rehabilitative and accountability based programs. Nevertheless, over the years the juvenile justice system has trended away from rehabilitation. Instead, over the past few decades, the system has increasingly incorporated measures that emphasize holding juveniles accountable for their actions. For example, during the 1990s, 47 states and the District of Columbia enacted laws that made their juvenile justice systems more punitive.[58] As a result, juvenile justice can be conceptualized as a continuum that stretches philosophically *from* the rehabilitative idea that juveniles are wayward youth who can be taught to mend their ways and become contributing members of society *to* the accountability end of the spectrum which holds that juveniles must be taught to take responsibility for their actions through punishment (often in the form of graduated sanctions).

The federal juvenile justice system can thus be viewed as a pendulum that swings between these two poles; over the past 20 years, it has clearly been swinging away from rehabilitation and toward accountability through the *addition* of graduated sanctions to the JJDPA State Formula grant program's purpose areas and the *requirement* that states implement graduated sanctions in order to be eligible for JABG funding. Congress may consider whether the federal government, through its grant programs, should be focusing on rehabilitating juveniles, holding them accountable for their actions, or some combination of both of these philosophies. As mentioned, authorization for the JABG expired at the end of FY2009. One of the current issues surrounding its potential reauthorization involves whether grant program purpose areas should be modified, expanded, or clarified.

Expanding or Modifying the JJDPA Core Mandates

The federal government has attempted to influence the states' juvenile justice systems through the core mandates that states must comply with in order to be eligible for funding. In essence, the federal government has used grant funding as a carrot to effectuate changes in the way that states house and treat their juvenile offenders. The last modification of a core mandate occurred with the JJDPA's last reauthorization in 2002, when the disproportionate minority contact language was modified to preclude OJJDP from using numerical benchmarks in its implementation. A possible issue for Congress to consider is whether to modify or expand the existing core mandates.

Proponents of expanding the core mandates could point to the fact that the mandates have been effective in inducing states to promulgate detention standards that focus on minimizing the contact between juvenile offenders and adults and in deinstitutionalizing status offenses.[59] Opponents of expanding the mandates, however, could point to the relative ineffectiveness of the disproportionate minority contact mandate; most states continue to detain minorities at a higher rate than their percentage of the state's juvenile population and the language has been weakened over the years to ensure that

OJJDP does not require states to meet quotas in order to adhere to the mandate.[60] Should Congress choose to expand the core mandates, policy options could include

- requiring states to ensure that their delinquency prevention programs are based on solid scientific evidence such as randomized control trials,[61]
- requiring states to show that they are reducing the disproportionate minority contact of offenders in the juvenile justice system as well as reducing the disproportionate number of minority juveniles transferred to adult courts,[62]
- expanding the number and quality of programs available for female juveniles,[63] or
- requiring states to implement mental health and substance abuse screening and treatment for juveniles.[64]

Juvenile Delinquency Prevention Block Grant

Since the JJDPA was reauthorized in 2002, there appears to have been some disparity between the authorizing legislation and the structure of the appropriations for some juvenile justice grant programs. As previously noted, this last reauthorization eliminated a number of small grant programs and consolidated most of their purpose areas into the Juvenile Delinquency Prevention Block Grant. However, the annual appropriation for OJJDP continues to follow the previous structure, and funds have been appropriated in each subsequent fiscal year for some of the grant programs that were repealed in 2002. The current disconnect between the authorization and the appropriation could present a challenge for OJJDP. Given this inconsistency, OJJDP employees must spend some percentage of their time reconciling the differences between the authorization and the appropriation; this may not represent the best investment of OJJDP staff time.

Additionally, because the eligibility requirements and funding mechanisms of the old grant programs and the new block grant program are different, this disparity between the authorization and the appropriation likely represents a challenge to the states and units of local government as they apply for funding. A potential issue for Congress as it reauthorizes the JJDPA includes whether the Juvenile Delinquency Prevention Block Grant should be implemented as it was authorized, whether it should be modified, or whether it should be broken up again into its component grant programs to better reflect what has been occurring with the appropriation.

Overlap in Grant Programs

The current grant programs within the JJDPA overlap in a variety of ways. The State Formula Grant and the Delinquency Prevention Block Grant programs, for example, both feature a wide array of purpose areas elucidated in legislative language that are largely similar. For example, both grant programs include purpose areas for

- counseling, mentoring, and training programs;
- community based programs and services;
- after school programs;
- education programs;
- programs that expand the use of probation officers;
- substance and drug abuse prevention programs;
- mental health services;
- gang-involvement prevention programs; and
- coordinating local service delivery among the different agencies involved.

Additionally, the Delinquency Prevention Block Grant, the Challenge Grants, and the Title V Incentive Grants for Local Delinquency Prevention Programs all include language allowing OJJDP to provide funding for additional programs not included in the specific purpose areas identified. A potential issue for Congress could include whether the current overlap within the juvenile justice grant programs is appropriate. Possible policy options could include altering the current grant programs to target funding for specific activities in each grant program or consolidating the different grant programs into one large program.

The creation of new grant programs could be an alternative to modifying or consolidating the existing grant programs. Creating grant programs that are tailored to specific activities (e.g., gang-prevention, restorative justice, mentoring, mental health treatment, etc.) could provide dedicated funding streams to activities that may not otherwise receive funding if they must compete for funding in a broader grant program. However, there are limited federal resources in the juvenile justice arena, and adding grant programs without also increasing funding may take resources away from the current programs. A possible issue for Congress involves whether the existing grant programs are adequate, whether the existing grant programs should be modified, or whether new grant programs should be enacted.

Coordination of Federal Efforts

The juvenile population comes into contact with a wide variety of federal programs overseen by a number different agencies. Under current law, the Administrator of OJJDP has a broad mandate to coordinate the federal government's overall response to juvenile offenders and juvenile delinquency prevention, including federal programs that focus on prevention, diversion, training, treatment, rehabilitation, evaluation, research, and improvement of the states' juvenile justice systems. Additionally, the Coordinating Council was established to help the various agencies involved in dealing with and providing treatment for juveniles better coordinate their efforts.

Some overlap exists within the federal government concerning programs that offer services for juveniles. For example, a growing body of evidence points to the relationship between child abuse or other forms of mistreatment and juvenile delinquency or other delinquent behavior such as youth violence.[65] This has led to a duplication of efforts within many federal agencies and what may sometimes be a considerable overlap in the funding opportunities available to states and local entities.[66] An example of this overlap is the body of federal funding available for youth violence prevention. Funding for youth violence programs is available within DOJ, the Department of Health and Human Services, the Department of Education, the Department of Labor, and the Department of Agriculture. Within these diverse departments, youth violence prevention funding opportunities are available for virtually every aspect of the issue: the violent youth themselves, their victims, their families, the communities they live in, the juvenile justice system that prosecutes them, and the societal factors that contribute to the violence.[67] In effect, there are a multitude of federal programs throughout the government that deal with youth violence's causes, its effects, and its ramifications. The amount of coordination that is occurring between the departments on these issues remains an open question.

Given the nexus between youth violence and juvenile justice, the coordination of these federal government programs should lie within the province of OJJDP and the Coordinating Council. The Coordinating Council, for its part, meets quarterly (for three to four hours on average) to discuss the ongoing juvenile justice related efforts within the agencies.[68] Given the extent of the overlap that exists within the federal government, some could question whether more coordination should be required across departments. A potential issue for Congress could involve how effective OJJDP and the Coordinating Council have been in coordinating the federal efforts to reduce juvenile delinquency, including efforts to address youth violence, in order to more efficiently provide treatment and services to juvenile offenders.

APPENDIX A. THE JUVENILE JUSTICE AND DELINQUENCY PREVENTION ACT (JJDPA) OF 1974

The Juvenile Justice and Delinquency Prevention Act (JJDPA) was first passed by Congress in 1974[69] and was most recently reauthorized in 2002 by the 21st Century Department of Justice Appropriations Authorization Act.[70] Its provisions are currently authorized through FY2007. This appendix will analyze the original JJDPA.

The original JJDPA had three main components: it created a set of institutions within the federal government that were dedicated to coordinating and administering federal juvenile justice efforts; it established grant programs to assist the states with setting up and running their juvenile justice systems; and it promulgated core mandates that states had to adhere to in order to be eligible to receive grant funding. As it was passed in 1974, the JJDPA focused largely on preventing juvenile delinquency and on rehabilitating juvenile offenders.

Federal Government Entities Established

The JJDPA established a range of federal government entities charged with overseeing the federal government's juvenile justice efforts that continue to exist today. In addition to establishing the first federal agency dedicated to the promulgation of juvenile justice, the act established a series of institutions aimed at increasing the federal government's coordination of juvenile delinquency programs and of programs that affect juveniles generally.

The Office of Juvenile Justice and Delinquency Prevention (OJJDP)

Title II, Part A of the original JJDPA established OJJDP within DOJ's Law Enforcement Assistance Administration (LEAA) as the new clearing house for federal juvenile justice efforts. The act established the Office of the Assistant Administrator of OJJDP, who is charged with overseeing the Office and coordinating the federal government-wide juvenile justice efforts under the direction of the Administrator of the LEAA. The act endowed the Administrator with a series of powers, including the authority to require other federal entities with juvenile delinquency programs to submit information and reports to OJJDP, and charged the new entity with administering the programs that were created by the act. The act also directed the Administrator to implement the overall policy and develop the objectives and priorities for *all* federal juvenile delinquency activities as well as "all activities relating to prevention, diversion, training, treatment, rehabilitation, evaluation, research, and improvement of the juvenile justice system of the United States."[71] The LEAA Administrator, acting through the OJJDP Assistant Administrator, was thus given a broad mandate to oversee and coordinate not just the new agency's activities but all federal activities relating to the treatment of juveniles. OJJDP was required to present Congress with an annual report of its activities and of the federal government's overall juvenile delinquency programs.

Coordinating Council on Juvenile Justice and Delinquency Prevention (Coordinating Council)

The act established an independent organization known as the Coordinating Council on Juvenile Justice and Delinquency Prevention to coordinate the federal government's juvenile delinquency programs. The Coordinating Council was to be comprised of representatives from a broad range of federal agencies who "exercise significant decision making authority in the Federal agency involved,"[72] including the Attorney General, Secretary of Health, Education, and Welfare, the Secretary of Labor, Director of the Special Action Office for Drug Abuse Prevention, Secretary of Housing and Urban Development, or their respective designees. Additionally, the Coordinating Council was to include the Assistant Administrator of OJJDP and the Deputy Assistant Administrator of the National Institute for Juvenile Justice and Delinquency Prevention. The Coordinating Council was to meet a minimum of six times per year and was to report its activities as part of OJJDP's annual report.

Advisory Committee on Juvenile Justice and Delinquency Prevention (Advisory Committee)

The act established an Advisory Committee composed of 21 individuals who were to be appointed by the President to serve in an advisory capacity. These individuals were to be experts in the fields of juvenile delinquency prevention or treatment; juvenile justice administration; or community based programs and private voluntary organizations. The majority of the Advisory Committee was to be drawn from the private sector and at least one-third of the members were to be younger than 26 at the time of their appointment. The members were to serve without compensation and to meet no less than four times a year. The Advisory Committee was charged with making recommendations to the Administrator of OJJDP concerning the planning, policies, priorities, operations, and management of all juvenile delinquency programs within the federal government.

The National Institute for Juvenile Justice and Delinquency Prevention (National Institute)

The act created the National Institute to coordinate the collection, preparation, and dissemination of data regarding the treatment and control of juvenile offenders. The National Institute was charged with serving as a clearing house for all information relating to juvenile delinquency and with conducting and encouraging research on juvenile delinquency. The National Institute was also charged with training juvenile justice practitioners from every level of government and the private sector who were connected with the treatment and control of juvenile offenders. The National Institute was endowed with the power to request other federal agencies to supply the data and statistics that were necessary for its mission, and to reimburse these agencies for the expenses associated with these requests.

Federal Grant Programs for Juvenile Justice

In addition to creating entities charged with overseeing and developing the juvenile delinquency prevention programs within the federal government, the JJDPA created two main grant programs that were aimed at helping states build up and manage their juvenile justice systems and prevent juvenile delinquency. Additionally, the JJDPA created a grant program aimed at helping states handle runaway youth.

Formula Grant Program

The first federal grant program established by the JJDPA was a formula grant program for states and local governments. This formula grant program was broadly aimed at helping states improve their juvenile justice systems by providing funding that could be used to assist in the planning, establishing, operating, coordinating, and evaluating of juvenile delinquency programs. Funding under this grant program was to be allocated to states based on their relative populations of people under the age of 18, and no state was to receive less than $200,000.[73] To receive funding under this grant program, the states were required to submit plans for how they were going to disburse the funding. The state plans were to describe a series of steps that states were to take in order to be eligible for funding, including the creation of juvenile justice entities within the state systems. States were required to pass along two-thirds of the funding to local government programs, unless granted a waiver by the Administrator, and 75% of the funds expended by the states were to be "used for advanced techniques in developing, maintaining, and expanding programs and services designed to prevent juvenile delinquency, to divert juveniles from the juvenile justice system, and to provide community based alternatives to juvenile detention and correctional facilities."[74]

In addition to these restrictions on how the money was to be spent, the JJDPA established two core mandates that states had to adhere to in order to receive funding. The first of these mandates required states to ensure that juveniles who had committed offenses that would not be crimes if they were committed by an adult (known as status offenses) not be placed in juvenile detention or correctional facilities. This has become known as the deinstitutionalization of status offenders. The second mandate required states to ensure that juveniles were not detained or confined in any institution in which they would have regular contact with adults in the criminal justice system.

Prevention and Treatment Programs Grant

The act authorized the Administrator to make grants to and enter into contracts with public and private agencies, organizations, institutions, and individuals that focused on delinquency prevention and treatment. The act authorized the Administrator to enter into these grants and contracts to, among other things, develop and implement new approaches and methods for juvenile delinquency programs; develop and maintain community based alternatives to institutionalization; develop and implement programs that diverted juveniles from the traditional correctional system; improve the delivery of services to delinquents and to at-risk youth; and implement programs aimed at keeping students in school.

Demonstration Programs Grant

The JJDPA also created a discretionary grant program aimed at supporting "innovative approaches to youth development and the prevention and treatment of delinquent behavior."[75] Grants under this program could be awarded to any state or local government agency, as well as nonprofit organizations, and were to last one year. The overarching goal of the program was to foster innovation in youth development.

APPENDIX B. SUBSEQUENT REVISIONS TO THE JJDPA

Between 1974 and 2001, there were a number of laws enacted that modified the JJDPA in some manner. This appendix will outline the main changes that were made to the JJDPA over the past three decades.

The Juvenile Justice Amendments of 1980 (P.L. 96-509)

In 1980, Congress made three major changes to the JJDPA and reauthorized the act through FY1984. One of the major changes enacted by P.L. 96-509 was the streamlining of the juvenile justice apparatus within DOJ; whereas the JJDPA placed OJJDP underneath the Law Enforcement Assistance Administration (LEAA) and gave the LEAA Administrator authority over the agency, under the new act's provisions the Administrator of OJJDP reported directly to the Attorney General. In essence, this gave OJJDP a measure of independence and removed the filter between the administrator of OJJDP and the Attorney General. Despite this, however, OJJDP remained administratively within LEAA. Another major change made to the JJPDA was the creation of a new core mandate that states were to adhere to in order to receive funding under the formula grant program: the removal of juveniles from adult jails and lockups. P.L. 96-509 also began the process of shifting the JJDPA's focus away from rehabilitation and towards sanctions, including language that called for OJJDP to focus additional attention on the problem of juveniles committing serious crimes by paying special attention to sentencing and adding resources to the juvenile court system.

The act also made a series of minor modifications to the Coordinating Council, the Advisory Committee, and the National Institute aimed at increasing the coordination of federal juvenile justice efforts and at including the perspective of juveniles into the process. Among the changes made to the JJPDA, the act allowed 7.5% of OJJDP's overall appropriation to be used for the concentration of federal juvenile delinquency efforts,[76] and it added the Director of the Bureau of Prisons, the Commissioner of the Bureau of Indian Affairs, the Commissioner for the Administration for Children, Youth, and Families, and the Director of the Youth Development Bureau to the Coordinating Council. The act directed the Advisory Committee to include at least five individuals younger than 24 years of age, at least two of whom should have been or continue to be under the jurisdiction of the juvenile justice system, and to contact and seek regular input from juveniles currently under the jurisdiction of the juvenile justice system.

The main alteration made by the act was the new requirement that states stop detaining or confining juveniles in any jail or lockup for adults in order to be eligible for the state formula grant. The act did, however, allow for the temporary detention of juveniles accused of serious crimes in such facilities where no existing acceptable alternative placement was possible, subject to the promulgation of regulations by the Administrator. Failure to achieve compliance with this mandate within five years would terminate a state's ability to receive funding unless the Administrator determined that the state was in substantial compliance with the requirements. Substantial compliance was defined as a state's achieving the removal of not less than 75% of juveniles from adult jails and lockups, and making an unequivocal commitment to achieving full compliance within two additional years.

The act also expanded the scope of the Prevention and Treatment Programs Grant to include programs that were aimed at removing juveniles from adult jails and lockups, and provided that at least 5% of the funding available under this grant program be allocated to the Virgin Islands, Guam, American Samoa, the Trust Territory of the Pacific Islands, and the Commonwealth of the Northern Mariana Islands.

The Juvenile Justice, Runaway Youth, and Missing Children's Act Amendments of 1984 Act (P.L. 98-473)

P.L. 98-473 reauthorized the JJDPA through FY1988 and formally elevated OJJDP to a standalone office within DOJ under the general authority of the Attorney General. Another major change made to the JJDPA by this act was the expansion of the Prevention and Treatment Programs Grant program. The act dedicated 15% to 25% of the overall funding for state formula grants to this program, and expanded the number of purpose areas that this discretionary grant could be used for, including, but not limited to, community based alternatives to detention; diversion mechanisms including restitution and reconciliation projects; advocacy activities aimed at improving services; programs that strengthen families; prevention and treatment programs; developing a national education program aimed at reducing juvenile delinquency; developing programs aimed at fostering youth employment; and developing programs aimed at keeping youths in school. At least 30% of the funding available under this program was to be apportioned to private nonprofit agencies and institutions.

The Amendments to the Juvenile Justice and Delinquency Prevention Act of 1988 (P.L. 100-690)

In 1988, Congress reauthorized the JJDPA through FY1992. Among other things, the act required OJJDP to publish a comprehensive plan of the activities it would undertake each year in the federal register. It also required OJJDP to prepare an annual report each fiscal year providing a detailed summary and analysis of the national trends in juvenile justice, including the numbers and types of offenses with which juveniles were being charged; the rate at which juveniles were being taken into custody; the extent to which states were complying with their state plan requirements; and OJJDP and the Coordinating Council's activities. The act also required states, as part of their plans, to include information on their efforts to end the disproportionate confinement of minority youth in their detention systems, and it raised the minimum funding allocations available for states under the formula grant program. The act also directed OJJDP to include technical assistance as a purpose area for each of its grant programs and for the National Institute. The act modified the Prevention and Treatment Programs Grant program by deleting language inserted by P.L. 98-473 that required 15% to 25% of the formula grant funding be allocated to this program and by expanding the number and types of considerations required to approve applications for funding.

Gang Prevention Grant

P.L. 100-690 also established a new grant program under Part D of Title II of the JJDPA aimed at funding prevention and treatment programs for juvenile gang members. The new discretionary grant program authorized the Administrator to make grants to public and private agencies and organizations. The new grant program identified 10 broad purpose areas aimed at reducing the numbers of juveniles joining gangs and providing treatment for juveniles convicted of gang-related criminal activities.

The Juvenile Justice and Delinquency Prevention Amendments Act of 1992 (P.L. 102-586)

P.L. 102-586 reauthorized the JJDPA through FY1996. The main change enacted by this act was the elevation of disproportionate minority confinement to core mandate status. States that were not in compliance with this requirement within three years of the act's passage would no longer be eligible for formula grant funding. However, states that had shown "substantial compliance" with the requirement would be eligible for funding for two additional years. The act created a number of new grant programs within Title II of the JJDPA, including grants for community-based gang intervention, for state challenge activities, for juvenile victims of child abuse, and for mentoring. The act also added a new Title V to the JJDPA establishing a new program, the Incentive Grants for Local Delinquency Prevention Program.

The act also modified the composition of the Coordinating Council. In addition to the leaders (or their designated representatives) of the various federal agencies with a stake in the juvenile justice system, the Coordinating Council was to include nine individuals working in the field of juvenile justice who were not federal employees. They were to be appointed without regard to political affiliation. Three members were to be appointed by the President, three by the Speaker of the House, and three by the majority leader of the Senate.

Following is a description of the various grant programs that were implemented by the 1992 revision to the JJDPA.

Community Based Gang Intervention Grant

The act slightly modified the discretionary gang prevention grant authorized within Part D of Title II of the JJDPA by P.L. 100-690, renaming it the Gang-Free Schools and Communities Grant. The act also created a new grant program, the Community-Based Gang Intervention Grant. The new grant program authorized the Administrator to make grants to public and private nonprofit agencies, organizations, and institutions to reduce the participation of juveniles in gangs by engaging the community. The grant allowed funding to be provided for coordinating mechanisms such as regional task-forces, as well as for a variety of prevention and accountability measures. For example, on the accountability side the grant authorized funding for graduated sanctions, including the expanded use of a wide variety of interventions such as probation, mediation, restitution, community service, intensive supervision, electronic monitoring, and bootcamps, among others. On the prevention side the program authorized funding for, among other things: treatment for juvenile gang members; prevention and treatment services for substance abuse by juveniles; and services to prevent juveniles from coming into contact with the juvenile justice system again as a result of gang-related activity.

State Challenge Activities Grant

The act created another new grant program under Part E of Title II of the JJDPA, the State Challenge Activities Grant (Challenge Grant). The Challenge Grant program allowed the Administrator to designate up to 10% of a state's formula grant for this new grant program. The act defined a challenge activity as a program that is aimed at, among other things, developing policies to provide services for juveniles in the juvenile justice system; increasing community-based alternatives to detention; developing programs that replaced traditional training schools with secure settings; developing programs that prohibited gender bias within the state's juvenile justice system and ensured that female juveniles had access to a full range of services, including treatment for physical or sexual assault and education in parenting; and increasing aftercare services for juveniles coming out of placement.

Juvenile Victims of Child Abuse Grant

The act created a third new grant program under Part F of Title II of the JJDPA for Juvenile Victims of Child Abuse. This program enabled the Administrator to enter into grants with public agencies and private nonprofit organizations to provide treatment for juvenile offenders who are victims of child abuse and neglect; provide transitional services, including individual, group, and family counseling; and carry out research on juvenile child abuse issues associated with these grants.

Juvenile Mentoring Grant

The act created a fourth new grant program under Part G of Title II of the JJDPA for juvenile mentoring programs. These grants could be awarded to local educational agencies (in partnership with public or private agencies) to establish and support mentoring programs. Mentoring programs eligible for funding included programs designed to link at-risk youth with responsible adults; promote personal and social responsibility; increase educational participation; discourage the use of drugs and violence; discourage participation in gangs; and encourage participation in community service and other community activities. Grant funding could not be used to directly compensate mentors (apart from reimbursement for incidental expenses) or support litigation of any kind, among other things.

Boot Camp Grants

The act created a fifth new grant program under Part H of Title II of the JJDPA to fund the establishment of up to 10 military-style boot camps in one or more states. These boot camps were to provide highly regimented schedules involving discipline, physical training, work, and drill, and to include educational and counseling services. States receiving funding under this program would be required to provide for post-release supervision and after-care services for the juveniles participating in their boot camps.

Incentive Grants for Local Delinquency Prevention Programs (Incentive Grants)

The act created a new Title V within the JJDPA for Incentive Grants aimed at creating delinquency prevention programs at the local level. The grants would be allocated by state and passed along by each state's advisory group (as created under the state plan stipulations) to local government entities. Funding could be used to provide recreation services, tutoring and remedial education, job skills, mental health services, substance abuse services, leadership development services, and programs that teach juveniles accountability for their actions. States were required to provide a 50% match for the grants and be in compliance with the core mandates in Title II in order to receive funding under this program.

The 21st Century Department of Justice Appropriations Authorization Act of 2002 (P.L. 107-273)

P.L. 107-273 in 2002 represents the last major revision to the JJDPA. The act reauthorized OJJDP, which had remained unauthorized since FY1997 but which had been appropriated annually, through FY2007. The act also made some significant revisions to the JJDPA, most notably repealing all of the new grant programs in Title II created by P.L. 102-586 and consolidating their purpose areas within the Juvenile Justice and Delinquency Prevention Block Grant.

Among other things, the act amended the state plans section of the JJDPA and modified the disproportionate minority confinement core mandate provision. The revision to the core mandate directed the states to address the problem of disproportionate minority confinement, but stated that the states were not required to meet numerical quotas or standards in order to receive formula grant funding. The act also mandated that states enact policies requiring that individuals who work with both juveniles and adults in detention facilities be certified and trained to work with juveniles. In addition, the act added a number of additional stipulations to the state plans, including, among other things,

- that states notify appropriate public agencies within 24 hours of a child's apprehension for a status offense;
- that states specify up to 5% of their formula grant funding for incentive grants to reduce probation officer case loads; and
- that states establish systems and policies to incorporate child protective services records into juvenile case files and to ensure that child welfare records are available to the court.

If states failed to comply with any of the four core mandates they would have their formula grant funding reduced by not less than 20% for each mandate with which they were not in compliance. Additionally, states would be ineligible to receive any formula funding unless they agreed to spend 50% of the funding they received on achieving compliance with whichever core mandate they were non-compliant with, unless the Administrator determined that the state had achieved substantial compliance with the mandate.

Juvenile Delinquency Prevention Block Grant

Perhaps the major structural change enacted by P.L. 107-273 was the elimination of the series of grant programs that had been created within Title II of the JJDPA: the Gang-Free Schools and Communities Grant; the Community Based Gang Intervention Grant; the States Challenge Activities Grant; the Juvenile Victims of Child Abuse Grant; the Juvenile Mentoring Grant; and the Boot Camps Grant. In their stead, the act created a Juvenile Delinquency Prevention Block Grant aimed at funding programs that reduced juvenile delinquency that incorporated most of the general purpose areas that had been eligible for funding under the previous grant programs. Included under this broad umbrella were 25 purpose areas that run the gamut of juvenile delinquency prevention, including, but not limited to, treatment programs; counseling programs; educational programs; programs that expanded the use of probation officers; community-based programs; drug-prevention programs; and gang-prevention programs.

End Notes

[1] U.S. Department of Justice, Office of Juvenile Justice and Delinquency Prevention, *Juvenile Justice: A Century of Change*, National Report Series, December 1999, p. 2. Hereinafter referred to as OJJDP, *A Century of Change*.

[2] P.L. 87-274

[3] P.L. 90-445.

[4] U.S. Department of Justice, Office of Juvenile Justice and Delinquency Prevention, "The JJDP Act: A Second Look," *Juvenile Justice*, vol. II, no. 2, Fall/Winter 1995.

[5] Federal Interagency Forum on Child and Family Statistics 1998, *America's Children: Key National Indicators of Well-Being*, at http://www.childstats.gov/pdf/ac1998/ac_98.pdf.

[6] P.L. 93-415.

[7] OJJDP, *A Century of Change*, p. 5.

[8] Karen Hess and Robert Drowns, *Juvenile Justice*, 4th Ed., Thomas Wadsworth, Belmont, CA, 2004, p. 7. Hereinafter referred to as Hess and Drowns, *Juvenile Justice*.

[9] Grossberg, Michael, "Changing Conceptions of Child Welfare in the United States, 1020-1935," Chapter 1 in Margaret K. Rosenheim, Franklin E. Zimring, David S. Tanenhaus, and Bernardine Dorhn, eds., *A Century of Juvenile Justice*, University of Chicago Press, Chicago, IL, 2002, p. 6. Hereinafter referred to as *A Century of Juvenile Justice*, Ch. 1.

[10] U.S. Department of Justice, Office of Juvenile Justice and Delinquency Prevention, *Juvenile Offenders and Victims: 1999 National Report*, 1999, p. 86, available at http://www.ncjrs.org/html/ojjdp/nationalreport99/toc.html. Hereinafter referred to as OJJDP, *1999 National Report*.

[11] OJJDP, *1999 National Report*, p. 86.

[12] Hess and Drowns, *Juvenile Justice*, pp. 15-16.

[13] OJJDP, *1999 National Report*, p. 86.

[14] OJJDP, *1999 National Report*, p. 87.

[15] Hess and Drowns, *Juvenile Justice*, p. 18.

[16] National Commission on Law Observance and Enforcement, *Report on the Child Offender in the Federal System of Justice*, 1931, p. 2.

[17] H.Rept. 958, 72nd Cong., 1st. Sess. 2, accompanying the bill enacted as 47 Stat. 301 (1932).

[18] *A Century of Juvenile Justice*, Ch. 1, pp. 27-29.

[19] 52 Stat. 764 (1938), 18 U.S.C. 921 to 927 (1940 ed.).

[20] 64 Stat. 1086 (1950), 18 U.S.C. 5005 to 5026 (1952 ed.).

[21] Hess and Drowns, *Juvenile Justice*, p. 21.

[22] OJJDP, *A Century of Change*, p. 3.

[23] 387 U.S. 1, 87 S. Ct. 1428 (1967).

[24] Other Supreme Court rulings that have directly impacted juvenile justice include *Kent v. United States* (383 U.S. 541, 1966), *In re Winship* (397 U.S. 358, 1970), *McKeiver v. Pennsylvania* (403 U.S. 528, 1971), *Breed v. Jones* (421 U.S. 519, 1975), *Oklahoma Publishing Company v. District Court in and for Oklahoma City* (430 U.S. 308, 1977), *Smith v. Daily Mail Publishing Company* (443 U.S. 97, 1979), and *Schall v. Martin* (467 U.S. 253, 1984).

[25] P.L. 87-274.

[26] U.S. Department of Justice, Office of Juvenile Justice and Delinquency Prevention, "The JJDP Act: A Second Look," *Juvenile Justice*, Vol. II, No.2, Fall/Winter 1995, p.12.

[27] P.L. 90-445.

[28] P.L. 90-351.

[29] LEAA has since been succeeded by the Office of Justice Programs (OJP).

[30] U.S. Department of Justice, Office of Juvenile Justice and Delinquency Prevention, "The JJDP Act: A Second Look," *Juvenile Justice*, Vol. II, No.2, Fall/Winter 1995, p.13.

[31] U.S. Congress, House Committee on Education and Labor, *Juvenile Justice and Delinquency Prevention Amendments of 1977*, H.Rept. 95-313, pp. 35-36.

[32] P.L. 90-415.

[33] P.L. 107-273.

[34] LEAA was established to serve as a clearinghouse for channeling federal funding to state and local law enforcement agencies. LEAA gave states incentives to establish planning agencies and funded a wide variety of programs spanning from education and research to local crime control initiatives.

[35] 42 U.S.C. §5614.

[36] P.L. 93-415, §206(a-b).

[37] 42 U.S.C. §5616.

[38] The JJDPA required states to formulate juvenile justice plans and adhere to certain mandates in order to receive formula grant funding; see discussion below.

[39] 42 U.S.C. §5617.

[40] See 42 U.S.C. §5631.

[41] 42 U.S.C. §5671(a)(1).

[42] This entire section references 42 U.S.C. §5633.

[43] The make up of this group should include at least one local elected official, representatives from the various state agencies involved in preventing, responding to, and treating juvenile delinquency, and other individuals working or volunteering in the field. A majority of the advisory group cannot be employed by the federal, state, or local government, one fifth of the members must be younger than 24, and at least 3 of the members must be within the jurisdiction of the juvenile justice system. 42 U.S.C. §5633 (a)(3).

[44] Indian tribes must comply with the four core mandates in order to be eligible for funding.

[45] 42 U.S.C. §5633 (a)(9).

[46] 42 U.S.C. §5633 (c).

[47] The most common status offence is truancy.

[48] 42 U.S.C. §5651-5656.

[49] P.L. 107-273.

[50] See Appendix B for more information on the changes enacted by the 21st Century Department of Justice Appropriations Authorization Act, P.L. 107-273.

[51] The purpose areas noted here show the breadth of activities that can be funded through this grant program. There are 25 purpose areas in all, and the last purpose area authorizes funding for "other activities that are likely to prevent juvenile delinquency." 42 U.S.C. §5652. Although it was authorized through FY2007, this program has not received appropriations to date.

[52] 42 U.S.C. §5661-5662.

[53] 42 U.S.C. §5781-5784.

[54] JABG was codified within the Omnibus Crime Control and Safe Streets Act of 1968 (42 U.S.C. 3796ee); as such it resides outside the immediate purview of the JJDPA despite the fact that it is administered by OJJDP.

[55] Under this subheading, the word *state* refers to the 50 states as well as the District of Columbia and the Commonwealth of Puerto Rico. Additionally, the Virgin Islands, American Samoa, Guam, and the Northern Mariana Islands are collectively considered to be one state for the purposes of JABG allocations.

[56] Graduated sanctions should be designed so that sanctions are imposed on a juvenile for each delinquent offense and escalate in intensity with each subsequent, more serious, offense. There should be "sufficient flexibility" to allow for individualized sanctions and services for juvenile offenders. Additionally, "appropriate consideration" should be given to public safety and the victims of the crime. 42 U.S.C. §3796ee-2(d).

[57] Violent crimes under this section include murder, non-negligent manslaughter, forcible rape, robbery, and aggravated assault.

[58] OJJDP, *A Century of Change*, p. 5.

[59] See Office of Juvenile Justice and Delinquency Prevention, *The Mandates*, Fact Sheet, March 1994, at http://www.ncjrs.gov/txtfiles/fs-9407.txt.

[60] See Eileen Poe-Yamagata and Michael A. Jones, *And Justice for Some*, Building Blocks for Youth, at http://www.buildingblocksforyouth.org/justiceforsome/jfs.pdf.

[61] For more information on the uses of randomized control trials evaluate government programs, see archived CRS Report RL33301, *Congress and Program Evaluation: An Overview of Randomized Controlled Trials (RCTs) and Related Issues*, by Clinton T. Brass, Erin D. Williams, and Blas Nuñez-Neto.

[62] See the Federal Advisory Committee on Juvenile Justice, *Final Summary Report of the 2009 Request for Information*, August 2009, http://www.facjj.org/annualrequest.html. Hereinafter referred to as FACJJ 2009 Report.

[63] U.S. Department of Justice, Office of Justice Programs, Office of Juvenile Justice and Delinquency Prevention, *How OJJDP is Serving Children, Families, and Communities*, NCJ 225036, 2008, http://www.ncjrs.gov/pdffiles1/ojjdp/ 225036.pdf.

[64] FACJJ 2009 Report.

[65] While some studies show smaller effect sizes for the link between child abuse and youth violence than others, there is nevertheless a significant correlation between the maltreatment of juveniles and subsequent delinquent or violent behavior. U.S. Public Health Service,

Office of the Surgeon General, *Youth Violence: A Report of the Surgeon General's Office*, 2001, pp. 65-72.

[66] See, for example, Janet Wiig with John A. Tuell, *Guidebook for Juvenile Justice and Child Welfare System Coordination and Integration*, Child Welfare League of America, 2004.

[67] From a CRS Congressional Distribution Memo, *Federal Youth Violence Programs*, Blas Nuñez-Neto, Coordinator. Available upon request.

[68] See Coordinating Council on Juvenile Justice and Delinquency Prevention, *Meetings*, available at http://www.juvenilecouncil.gov/meetings.html.

[69] P.L. 90-415.

[70] P.L. 107-273.

[71] P.L. 93-415, §204(a).

[72] P.L. 93-415, §206(a-b).

[73] The Virgin Islands, Guam, American Samoa, and the Trust Territory of the Pacific Islands were to receive no less than $50,000.

[74] P.L. 93-415, §223(a)(10).

[75] P.L. 93-415, §401.

[76] This meant, in essence, that OJJDP could use 7.5% of the overall appropriation for its own administrative costs in ensuring that the grants that were awarded were effectively concentrating federal funding on the issues that were considered to be most important.

In: Juvenile Justice
Editor: Lana Traverso
ISBN: 978-1-63321-261-9

Chapter 2

JUVENILE JUSTICE ANNOTATED BIBLIOGRAPHY*

National Institute of Corrections Information Center

JUVENILE JUSTICE: COURTS

Advances in Juvenile Justice Reform: 2009-2011. Washington, DC: National Juvenile Justice Network, 2012.

This "document includes a wide array of youth justice reforms from across the country: significant new laws, administrative rule and practice changes, positive court decisions, and promising commissions and studies". Reforms are organized according to these issue areas: Adjudication and Sentencing; Alternatives to Detention and Youth Prisons; Competency; Conditions of Confinement; Confidentiality and Expungement; Disproportionate Minority Contact (DMC); Facility Closures and Downsizing; Gangs; Girls in the System; Immigrant Youth in the System; International Standards; Interrogations and Confessions; Juvenile Defense and Court Process; Lesbian, Gay, Bisexual, Transgender, and Questioning Youth in the System; Mental Health and Substance Abuse; Organizational and Large-Scale Change; Probation, Parole, and Reentry; School-to-Prison Pipeline; Screening and Assessment; Sex Offender Laws and Registries; Sexual Exploitation of

* This is an edited, reformatted and augmented version of a document dated January 2014.

Youth; Status Offenses; Youth in the Adult System; and Youth Involved in the Juvenile Justice and Child Welfare Systems. These reforms are also organized according to state.
http://www.njjn.org/our-work/juvenile-justice-reform-advances-2009-2011?utmsource=Eblast%3A+Advances+in+Juvenile+Justice+Reform%3A2009-2011&utmcampaign=Advances+Bulletin+-+Sept+20%2C+2012&utmmedium=email http://nicic.gov/Library/026565

Bench Book for Judges & Court Personnel. (Version 1.0). Lexington, KY: Interstate Commission for Juveniles, 2011.
The role, rules, and processes of the Interstate Compact for Juveniles (ICJ) are explained. The ICJ governs the interstate movement of juveniles. Sections prior to the five chapters are: latest development in the Interstate Compact for Juveniles, how to use this Bench Book, introduction, and Quick Reference Guide. Chapters include: understanding interstate compacts and the general law of interstate compacts; the Interstate Compact for Juveniles; the revised ICJ and its implications for the courts; returning juveniles; and liability and immunity considerations for judicial officers and employees. Appendixes provide the following: model legislation; by-laws; rules; advisory opinions of the Interstate Commission for Juveniles; Notice of Clarification of the Office of Juvenile Justice and Delinquency Prevention (OJJDP) Policy on Secure Detention of Runaways; and process charts.
http://www.juvenilecompact.org/LinkClick.aspx?fileticket=hP5YtZN5GWU=&tabid=969 http://nicic.gov/Library/024959

Butts, Jeffrey A. Transfer of Juveniles to Criminal Court is Not Correlated with Falling Youth *Violence*. New York: John Jay College of Criminal Justice/Research and Evaluation Center, 2012.
"At first glance, it may appear that the greater use of transfer lowered violent youth crime, but this argument is refuted by a simple analysis of crime trends. In the six states that allow fair comparisons (i.e., where all juveniles ages 16-17 are originally subject to juvenile court jurisdiction and sufficient data exist for the calculations), the use of criminal court transfer bears no relationship to changes in juvenile violence". This brief goes on to explain why there is no connection between transfer and reduced rates of juvenile crime.
http://jeffreybutts.files.wordpress.com/2012/03/databit2012 051.pdf

Callahan, Lisa, Joseph Cocozza, Henry J. Steadman, and Sheila Tillman. "A National Survey of U.S. Juvenile Mental Health Courts." *Psychiatric Services* 63, no. 2 (2012): 130-134.

Results from a survey of juvenile mental health courts (JMHCs) in the United States are presented. Information is provided regarding: program characteristics—parent agency responsible, access points, organizations involved with the court, funding source, and multidisciplinary team members; and participant characteristics—age, race, sex, current offenses, and most common diagnosis. JMHCs primarily operate under the juvenile court with funding from the state. Participant offenses are mostly misdemeanors with bipolar disorder being the prevalent diagnosis. The major challenge facing JMHCs is that they "are being developed in the absence of systematically collected outcome data" (p. 134).

http://gains.prainc.com/pdfs/jmhc/JMHCnat'lsurvey.pdf

Coalition for Juvenile Justice (CJJ). Positive Power: Exercising Judicial Leadership to Prevent Court Involvement and Incarceration of Non-Delinquent Youth. Washington, DC: SOS Project, 2012.

Strategies that judges can use for keeping youth identified as status offenders out of correctional institutions are illustrated through the practices of nine juvenile and family court judges. Sections of this brief include: introduction; defining the issue—first do no harm; exploring a solution—judicial leadership on the Deinstitutionalization of Status Offenders (DSO) core requirement of the federal Juvenile Justice and Delinquency Prevention Act (JJDPA); four elements of effective judicial leadership—demand for evidence-based approaches, balancing of interests, reliance on partnerships, and the use of judicial convening power; the nine judges and how they address status offenses; and expanding judicial leadership on DSO.

http://www.juvjustice.org/media/resources/public/resource 390.pdf

Dickerson, James G., Crystal Collins-Camargo, and Ramie Martin-Galijatovic. "How Collaborative the Collaboration? Assessing Interagency Collaboration within a Juvenile Court Diversion Program." *Juvenile & Family Court Journal* 63, no. 3 (June 2012): 21-35.

Juvenile delinquency with co-occurring substance abuse and mental health disorders has become an increasing problem within the United States. In part this can be attributed to the excessive number of delinquent youth entering the juvenile justice system with untreated substance abuse and/or mental health disorders. In an effort to combat this problem, interagency collaborations have been formed to provide more effective treatment services. One such interagency collaboration is the JETS Program. This study identifies the strengths and limitations of establishing an interagency collaboration within the first year of a juvenile treatment court's inception.

Driver, Christine, and Eve M. Brank. "Juveniles' Knowledge of the Court Process: Results from Instruction from an Electronic Source." *Behavioral Sciences & the Law* 27, no. 4 (Jul/Aug2009): 627-642.
Our study first determined what juveniles know about the juvenile court process. Second, it evaluated a DVD designed to be a systematic and simple way to improve this knowledge. A pre- and posttest design was used with two pilot samples and two samples from the population of interest. A sample from a juvenile detention center (n = 118) was the focus of this study. Initial knowledge of the court process was quite low for the detention sample (pretest M = 64.0%, SD = 14.2%). All samples experienced a significant improvement of knowledge after watching the DVD. Youth in the detention sample had a mean improvement from pretest to posttest of 6.4% (SD = 11.9%), with mean scores at posttest being 70.3% (SD = 17.4%). Respondents varied in their performance on different question topics, scoring the lowest on questions related to what happens at juvenile court hearings. The social and demographic variables of age, race, gender, grades in school, number of previous arrests, and the number of times the respondent had been to court were evaluated through regression analysis. Age and race were found to be significantly related to pretest scores, and race was significantly related to improvement scores.

Dvorchak, Kim, and Karina Swenson. Re-Directing Justice: The Consequences of Prosecuting Youth as Adults and the Need to Restore Judicial Oversight. Denver: Colorado Juvenile Defender Coalition, 2012.
The use of "direct filing," the prosecuting youth as adults, in Colorado is examined. This critical report shows how ineffective and costly direct filing is. Key findings from this study include: 1. Trying youth as adults doesn't make Colorado safer, but increases the likelihood a teenager will re-offend; 2. Direct file has affected thousands of youth, and the law disproportionately impacts black and Hispanic youth; 3. The vast majority of youth impacted by direct file are not the most serious offenders; 4. Most youth who enter the system as a result of Direct File do not see their case reviewed by a judge or jury, and are convicted of a lower offense

than their original charge; 5. Most youth prosecuted in adult courts await trial in adult jails, which are dangerously unequipped for youth; 6. Convicting youth as adults can expose them to all of the risks youth face in adult prisons, and carry long-term consequences that make it difficult to reintegrate into society; and 7. The Youthful Offender System has not been shown to be an effective intervention program, is costly, and its services and outcomes need to be better scrutinized (p. 1).
http://cjdc.org/wp/juvenile-justice-policy/re-directing-justice/

Fact Sheets. Campaign for Youth Justice (Washington, DC), 2012.
These fact sheets show how much harm is inflicted on youth prosecuted in adult courts. Twenty-three items are organized according to: key statistics about youth crime (Key Facts—Youth in the Justice System, Chart of Youth Arrests, and Chart of Declining Juvenile Crime Rates and Age-Specific Arrest Rates; youth tried as adults (How a Youth Ends Up in the Adult Justice System, Teen Brains Are Not Fully Developed, Adolescent Brain Development, Comparison of the Juvenile System to the Adult System, Education Needs of Youth in the Justice System, Youth Have Lifelong Barriers to Employment, Young Children in the Adult System, International Consensus Against Trying Youth As Adults, and Transfer Laws Did Not Cause Crime Decline; studies on recidivism (Prosecuting Youth in the Adult System Leads to More Crime, Not Less, Summary of Transfer Research Studies, Fact Sheet on OJJDP Transfer Bulletin, and Fact Sheet on CDC Study; dangers of housing youth in adult facilities (Key Facts--Youth in Adult Jails and Prisons, Why Youth Facilities Are Better Than Adult Facilities, Youth Housed in Adult Jails and Prisons, and Fact Sheet on CFYJ Report - Jailing Juveniles); and racial and ethnic disparities (Disproportionate Impact on Youth of Color, Impact on African-American Youth, Impact on Latino Youth, and Impact on Native American Youth. http://www.campaignforyouthjustice.org/fact-sheets.html
http://nicic.gov/Library/026394

Fair Sentencing for Youth. New York: Human Rights Watch, 2012.
Fair Sentencing for Youth is a growing, collaborative project powered by many groups and individuals. We believe youth deserve the chance to prove themselves." Access points are: cases and bills; take action; supporters; changed life; the facts—the need for change, international

consensus, the fiscal impact, adolescent development, and human rights law; about this organization; and Cares 4 Youth (California).
http://www.fairsentencingforyouth.org/
http://nicic.gov/Library/026571

Falling through the Cracks: A New Look at Ohio Youth in the Adult Criminal Justice System. Covington, KY Children's Law Center, Inc., 2012.
[R]ecent research shows that children face long-lasting harms during their time in the adult system and exit adult court more likely to commit a higher number of offenses, and more serious offenses, than similar youth who are retained in the juvenile justice system ... Although Ohio has taken a first step toward reducing youths' contact with the adult criminal justice system, Ohio law still allows many youth to become involved with the adult system. This report focuses on national research and trends regarding youth in the adult system, Ohio's laws on this issue, and a path forward for Ohio to more effectively respond to youth" (p. 1). This report contains these sections: introduction; research and national context on the effects of placing youth in the adult criminal justice system—trends away from the adultification of youth; children in the Ohio adult criminal justice system—tracks to adult courts how youth come into contact with the adult criminal justice system—bindover, serious youthful offender (SYO), and juvenile justice system involved youth after they turn 18), data and statistics on youth in Ohio's court systems; the history of Ohio's adultification laws; shifting directions in Ohio—research and policy behind keeping kids as kids; moving forward—recommendations; and conclusion.
http://www.campaignforyouthjustice.org/documents/FROH0512.pdf
http://nicic.gov/Library/026406

Frola, Margaret. "Low-Risk Youths Referred to Pima County Juvenile Court Center Detention Intake: Needs, Detention, and Recidivism." *Juvenile & Family Court Journal* 60, no. 3 (2009): 45-65.
Abstract: Delinquent youths who were low risk to re-offend were the subject of this study. It was hypothesized that these youths would have high levels of need (e.g., mental illness) and that detention would lead to increased recidivism. Demographic and social factors, delinquency history, and recidivism data were analyzed, producing four major findings: low-risk youths have high needs, low-risk youths recidivate at high rates, unaddressed needs increase the likelihood of detention and

recidivism, and behavioral health needs were among the strongest predictors of recidivism. The factors that lead to recidivism are discussed, and suggestions for improving outcomes are also presented. [ABSTRACT FROM AUTHOR]

Griffin, Patrick, Sean Addie, Benjamin Adams, and Kathy Firestine. *Trying Juveniles as Adults: An Analysis of State Transfer Laws and Reporting*. Washington, DC: Office of Juvenile Justice and Delinquency Prevention, 2011.

"In addition to providing the latest overview of state transfer laws and practices, this bulletin comprehensively examines available state-level data on juveniles adjudicated in the criminal justice system" (p. 1). Topics covered include: all states set age levels at where childhood ends and adult criminal responsibility begins; for every 1,000 petitioned delinquency cases, about 9 are waived to criminal court; most states do not track or account for all of their juvenile transfer cases; wide variations exist in how states document juvenile transfers; juveniles in most states can be jailed awaiting trial in criminal court; convicted juveniles do not always receive harsher sanctions in the adult system; and transfer laws generally have not been shown to deter crime.

https://www.ncjrs.gov/pdffiles1/ojjdp/232434.pdf

Investigation of the Shelby County Juvenile Court. U.S. Department of Justice. Washington, DC: Civil Rights Division, 2012.

Results from an investigation of operations by the Juvenile Court of Memphis and Shelby County (JCMSC) and the Shelby County Juvenile Detention Center are presented. These observations support the concerns some organizations have about the juvenile justice system in the United States. Sections following a summary of findings are: the investigation; background of juvenile courts; due process violations; equal protection and Title VI findings; practices that contribute to due process and equal protection violations; detention findings; and remedial measures. "We find that JCMSC fails to provide constitutionally required due process to children of all races. In addition, we find that JCMSC's administration of justice discriminates against Black children. Further, we find that JCMSC violates the substantive due process rights of detained youth by not providing them with reasonably safe conditions of confinement" (p. 1).

http://www.justice.gov/crt/about/spl/documents/shelbycountyjuvfindingsrpt4-26-12.pdf http://nicic.gov/Library/026265

Juvenile Mental Health Courts. Delmar, NY: GAINS Center for Behavioral Health and Justice Transformation, 2012.
"Juvenile Mental Health Courts (JMHCs) provide case management and support to youth in the juvenile justice system with behavioral health needs. These courts focus on treatment and rehabilitation, and help to divert youth from juvenile detention facilities to community-based services in their local systems of care." This website provides a map showing where JMHCs are located within the United States.
http://gainscenter.samhsa.gov/grant programs/juvenilemhc.asp

Larson, Kimberly, and Thomas Grisso. *Developing Statutes for Competence to Stand Trial in Juvenile Delinquency Proceedings: A Guide for Lawmakers.* Worcester, MA: National Youth Screening and Assessment Project; and Washington, DC: Models for Change, 2012.
This document has been prepared to assist states that are considering developing or amending statutes pertaining to competence to stand trial in juvenile court delinquency proceedings. The need for the development of statutes regarding the application of competence to stand trial (CST) in juvenile court proceedings arises from recent historical developments ... Nevertheless, most states have not yet developed statutory guidance for the application of CST in juvenile court proceedings" (p. 2). Sections of this guide are: introduction; background to CST in the criminal justice system and CST in the juvenile justice system; modules—definition of competence to stand trial, procedural issues, competence evaluations by mental health examiners, and remediation and legal disposition of incompetent juvenile defendants; summary of recommendations; and afterword—youth in criminal court.
http://www.modelsforchange.net/publications/330/DevelopingStatutesf or Competence to Stand Trial in Juvenile Delinquency Proceedings A Guide for Lawmakers.pdf

Miller v. Alabama. Certiorari to the Court of Criminal Appeals of Alabama. Washington, DC: United States Supreme Court, 2012.
"By requiring that all children convicted of homicide receive lifetime incarceration without possibility of parole, regardless of their age and age-related characteristics and the nature of their crimes, the mandatory sentencing schemes before us violate this principle of proportionality, and so the Eighth Amendment's ban on cruel and unusual punishment. We accordingly reverse the judgments of the Arkansas Supreme Court and

Alabama Court of Criminal Appeals and remand the cases for further proceedings not inconsistent with this opinion" (p. 27).
http://www.supremecourt.gov/opinions/11pdf/10-9646g2i8.pdf?utm source=BULLETIN%3A+Mandatory+Life+Without+Parole+Sentences+for+Juveniles+Banned&utmcampaign=Bulletin%3A+June+25%2C+2012&utm medium=email

Puzzanchera, Charles, and Benjamin Adams. *Juvenile Arrests 2009.* Washington, DC: U.S. Department of Justice/Office of Juvenile Justice and Delinquency Prevention, 2011.
This publication provides a "comprehensive statistical overview of the problems of juvenile crime, violence, and victimization and the response of the juvenile justice system" (p. 1). Data show that juvenile crime is not on the rise. Arrests of juveniles for violent offenses dropped 10% from 2008 to 2009. Since arrest rates hit their peak in 1994, there has been a decline of almost 50%. Yet, the juvenile arrest rate for simple assault, which is the most common juvenile crime against people, has risen 15% since 1980. http://ojjdp.gov/publications/PubAbstract.asp?pubi=258483
http://nicic.gov/Library/025518

Puzzanchera, Charles, Adams, Benjamin, and Sarah Hockenberry. *Juvenile Court Statistics 2009*. Pittsburgh, PA: National Center for Juvenile Justice, 2012.
Delinquency and status offense cases managed by U.S. courts with juvenile jurisdiction between 1985 and 2009 are analyzed and commented on. This report contains four chapters: introduction; national estimates of delinquency cases—counts and trends, case rates, age at referral, gender, and race; national estimates of delinquency case processing -- referral, detention, intake decision, waiver, adjudication, dispositions (out-of-home placement and probation), and case processing; and national estimates of petitioned status offense cases by counts and trends, case rates, age at referral, gender, race, source of referral, detention, adjudication, dispositions (out-of-home placement and probation), and case processing. Appendixes provide glossary of terms and reported juvenile court cases disposed in 2009 by county.

Puzzanchera, Charles, Benjamin Adams, and Melissa Sickmund. *Juvenile Court Statistics* 2008-2011. Pittsburgh, PA: National Center for Juvenile Justice.

Delinquency and status offense cases managed by U.S. courts with juvenile jurisdiction between 1985 and 2008 are analyzed and commented on. This report contains four chapters: introduction; national estimates of delinquency cases—counts and trends, case rates, age at referral, gender, and race; national estimates of delinquency case processing -- referral, detention, intake decision, waiver, adjudication, dispositions (out-of-home placement and probation), and case processing; and national estimates of petitioned status offense cases by counts and trends, case rates, age at referral, gender, race, source of referral, detention, adjudication, dispositions (out-of-home placement and probation), and case processing. Appendixes provide glossary of terms and reported juvenile court cases disposed in 2008 by county.
http://www.ncjj.org/pdf/jcsreports/jcs2008.pdf
http://nicic.gov/Library/025365

Rodriguez, Nancy. "The Cumulative Effect of Race and Ethnicity in Juvenile Court Outcomes and Why Pre-adjudication Detention Matters." *Journal of Research in Crime and Delinquency* 47, no. 3 (2010): 391-413.
Despite federal and state legislation aimed at producing equitable treatment of youth in the juvenile court system, studies continue to find that race and ethnicity play a significant role in juvenile court outcomes. To date, few studies have examined the cumulative effects of race and ethnicity in juvenile court outcomes. In this study, a random sample of youth processed in Arizona during 2000 (N 23,156) was used to examine how race and ethnicity influence diversion, petition, detention, adjudication, and disposition decisions. Analyses show that black, Latino, and American Indian youth were treated more severely in juvenile court outcomes than their white counterparts. Also, youth who were detained pre-adjudication were more likely to have a petition filed, less likely to have petitions dismissed, and more likely to be removed from the home at disposition. Implications for policy and practice are discussed. [Publication Abstract]
http://firstsearch.oclc.org/WebZ/DARead?key=0022-4278%252820100801%252947%253A3%253C391%253ATCEORA%253E%26fsapp8-51043-h9psrhlcuaah54%26205bc566b84ad76af22dc4d712ac747e041f30241095655e56bd0e0e326136a5&sessionid=0&db=ECO FT&format=PDF

Juvenile Assessment

Baglivio, Michael T. "The Assessment of Risk to Recidivate Among a Juvenile Offending Population." *Journal of Criminal Justice* 37, no. 6 (2009): 596-607.

The Florida Department of Juvenile Justice has implemented a new fourth-generation risk/need assessment to assess the risk to re-offend for juveniles referred to the department. The new assessment, the Positive Achievement Change Tool, or PACT, is adapted from the validated Washington State Juvenile Court Assessment, on which the Youth Assessment Screening Inventory (YASI) was also modeled. This study validated the PACT assessment, and examined whether the instrument is as predictive of female delinquency as it is of male delinquency, utilizing subsequent official delinquency referral as the dependent measure. Gender differences were explored and illustrated the instrument to be effective in predicting female and male delinquency, yet the factors predicting female delinquency did not mimic those predictive of male delinquency. Furthermore, for both male and female juveniles, a score of environmental and personal characteristics and situations had a stronger relationship with recidivism than did a score of official criminal history.

Baglivio, Michael T., and Katherine Jackowski. "Examining the Validity of a Juvenile Offending Risk Assessment Instrument across Gender and Race/Ethnicity." *Youth Violence & Juvenile Justice* 11, no. 1 (2013): 26-43.

Analysis of predictive validity of the risk/needs assessment used by a criminal justice agency is paramount. The validity of the Positive Achievement Change Tool (PACT) across gender/race/ethnicity in a juvenile sample was examined. Results demonstrate recidivism increases as PACT score increases, with minor exceptions. Findings suggest similar prediction of referral/arrest and adjudication/conviction across subgroups. 95% confidence intervals overlapped for all subgroups on 13 of 19 measures examined. However, which factors predict recidivism across subgroups differ. Criminal history was the most prevalent predictor, while no factor predicted White female offending. "Gender-responsive" item inclusion measuring abusive/traumatic circumstances did not improve prediction.

Bechtel, Kristin, Christopher T. Lowenkamp, and Edward Latessa. "Assessing the Risk of Re-Offending of Juvenile Offending for Juvenile Offenders Using the Youth Level of Service/Case Management Inventory." *Journal of Offender Rehabilitation* 45, no. 3/4 (2007): 85-108.

The purpose of the Youth Level of Service Case Management Inventory (YLS/CMI) is to assess, classify, and assist agencies with developing treatment and service plans according to the offender's criminogenic risk factors. Given the limited research in the predictive validity for this instrument, the current study attempts to examine this issue on a sample of 4,482 juveniles from Ohio who were given sentences in the community or to juvenile institutions. Results demonstrated the validity of the YLS/CMI in predicting recidivism for both settings.

http://www.uc.edu/content/dam/uc/ccjr/docs/articles/RiskofReoffendingYLSCMI.pdf

Benner, Gregory J., Scott A. Stage, Ron J. Nelson, Mike Laederich, and Nicole C. Ralston. "Predicting the Cumulative Recidivism of Juvenile Detainees." *Journal of Behavior Analysis of Offender & Victim: Treatment & Prevention* 2, no. 1 (2010): 51-62.

The primary purpose of this research was to identify the most robust set of factors contributing to the recidivism of juvenile detainees; including demographic, court history, mental health, substance abuse, and maltreatment variables. Recidivism in this paper is defined as having received more than one status offense or non-status offense. Status offenses are incurred because of the prohibition of various acts due to the offender's status as a juvenile (e.g., alcohol consumption, violation of curfew, or truancy). Non-status offenses (i.e., delinquency) are incurred because of violation of the law and commitment of a crime. The study population included 761 juvenile offenders in the Northwest. Juveniles who had a history of childhood maltreatment, above average use of alcohol/drugs, and experienced traumatic experiences were four times (4.22 odds ratio) more likely to have repeated juvenile status offenses. Further, sex and suicide ideation increased the likelihood of committed repeated non-status offenses by 6.5 times. Findings, limitations, and implications are discussed. [ABSTRACT FROM AUTHOR]

Brame, Robert, Michael G. Turner, Raymond Paternoster, and Shawn D. Bushway. Cumulative Prevalence of Arrest From Ages 8 to 23 in a National Sample [Abstract] (Pediatrics eFirst Early Release), 2012.

The prevalence of youth ages 8-23 years old who say they have been arrested or taken into custody for illegal or delinquent offenses (excluding minor traffic violations) is determined. Note this is self-report data. It appears that anywhere from 30.2% to 41.4% of youth by age 23 experienced some involvement with the criminal justice system. "The greatest growth in the cumulative prevalence of arrest occurs during late adolescence and the period of early or emerging adulthood." It should also be noted that not all of these encounters resulted in arrest or criminal conviction. NIC Accession Number: 025532
http://pediatrics.aappublications.org/content/early/2011/12/14/peds.2010 - 3710.abstract?sid=8ddc649f-01f5-431d-8aad-f878645c9650

Campaign for Youth Justice Youth Justice System Survey. GBA Strategies (Washington, DC), 2011.
The opinions of the general public regarding the juvenile justice system are determined. Topics covered are: key survey findings; focusing on rehabilitation and getting youth out of adult correctional facilities; beliefs about youth crime and the juvenile justice system; youth facilities vs. adult jails; the establishment of a minimum age to try youth in adult courts with decisions being made by judges; adult vs. juvenile court decided on a case-by-case basis; implementing key reforms to the juvenile justice system; proposals to reform the juvenile justice system; and proposals to reform the way parents and communities are involved.
http://www.gbastrategies.com/public files/cfyj101111m1.pdf
http://nicic.gov/Library/026492

Chambers, Benjamin. Doing it Right: Risk Assessment in Juvenile Justice – An NJJN Webinar.
Presenter: Gina Vincent, PhD, Co-Director of the National Youth Screening & Assessment Project.
http://www.njjn.org/article/doing-it-right-risk-assessment-in-juvenile-justice---an-njjn-webinar

Clayton, John. "Washington's Journey with Evidence-Based and Research-Based Programs in Juvenile Justice." *Policy & Practice* 70, no. 3 (2012): 20-22.
The article focuses on evidence-based and research-based programs that are part of juvenile justice in Washington and finding cost effective programs to reduce recidivism among juvenile offenders. The U.S.

Community Juvenile Accountability Act (CJAA) was passed by the Washington State Legislature to check if the programs reduce repeat offenses by juvenile offenders. A system of risk assessment has been implemented by county juvenile courts to identify levels of risk and eligibility of youths.

Dolan, Mairead, Troy E. McEwan, Rebekah Doley, and Katarina Fritzon. "Risk Factors and Risk Assessment in Juvenile Fire-Setting." *Psychiatry, Psychology & Law* 18, no. 3 (2011): 378-394.

This article provides an overview of the literature on risk issues in juvenile fire-setting behaviour. In particular, we highlight the importance of acknowledging the differences in terminology used in current studies and outline the importance of developmental issues in understanding when fire-related activities should be considered pathological. The estimated prevalence of fire interest, fire play, fire-setting and arson are discussed. The key sociodemographic, individual and environmental factors that are associated with pathological fire-setting are discussed in the context of general delinquency. The limited findings, to date, suggest that fire-setting in the main is similar to non-fire-setting delinquent behaviour in juveniles as the majority have conduct disorder rather than major mental illness. There is some very limited evidence that attentional problems may have a specific association with fire-setting but this requires replication on a larger scale. Risk assessment for those who have engaged in fire-setting behaviour is contextualised within the model outlined in the United States Federal Emergency Management Agency (FEMA) as this is one of the leading international agencies conducting work in this field. A variety of available risk assessment tools are outlined and the utility of FEMA models and screening tools for assigning cases to appropriate risk assessment-based interventions is outlined. Additional clinically based tools are discussed and their value in treatment/ management assignment decisions is highlighted. Using a risk model for fire-setting, it is clear that multiagency working is crucial in designating cases to higher levels of multi-disciplinary assessment and treatment. At present, current international and Australian interventions for juveniles largely focus on educational and fire safety awareness programmes and there is a lack of structured clinically based programmes that meet the needs of those higher-risk juveniles who have unmet mental health and social needs. [ABSTRACT FROM AUTHOR]

Edinburgh, Laurel. "The 10-Question Tool: A Novel Screening Instrument for Runaway Youth." *OJJDP Journal of Juvenile Justice* 1, no. 2 (2011): 80-94.

Adolescents who run away face high rates of sexual and physical assault, yet there are no established brief screening tools that police can use to determine adolescents' safety or that help police refer such youth to needed services when they are located. We developed the 10- Question Tool for law enforcement officers to screen run - away youth about issues related to their safety. We reviewed 300 10-Question forms completed by law enforcement officers in St. Paul, Minnesota. Our analyses explored demographic characteristics of runaway youth, including their reasons for leaving home, disclosure of injury, sexual assault, and their need for health care. This novel approach to screening by law enforcement officers appears to identify, locate, and refer runaway teens needing services as a result of myriad harms, including sexual assault.
http://www.journalofjuvjustice.org/JOJJ0102/ePub.htm

Egley, Arlen, Jr, Howell, James C. *Highlights of the 2009 National Youth Gang Survey.* Washington, DC: U.S. Dept. of Justice. Office of Juvenile Justice and Delinquency Prevention, 2011.

Those individuals concerned about juvenile gangs in the United States should read this review. Sections of this summary are: key points; survey findings for gang prevalence, gang activity, and gang homicides; and factors influencing local gang violence—drug-related, intergang conflict, and returning inmates.
http://www.ncjrs.gov/pdffiles1/ojjdp/233581.pdf
http://nicic.gov/Library/025083

Egley, Arlen, Jr., and James C. Howell. *Highlights of the 2010 National Youth Gang Survey.* Washington, DC: U.S. Department of Justice/Office of Juvenile Justice and Delinquency Prevention, 2012.

Those individuals concerned about juvenile gangs in the United States should read this review. Sections of this summary are: key points; survey findings for gang-related offenses, gang-member migration, and external gang influences; and conclusion. "The prevalence rate of gang activity remained relatively stable from 2005 to 2010, in contrast to the drop in overall crime over the past decade. In 2010, gang activity and serious gang crime remained highly concentrated in the most populated jurisdictions.

Nationally, gang-related homicides increased more than 10 percent from 2009 to 2010 in very large cities" (p. 4).
http://www.ojjdp.gov/pubs/237542.pdf

Emeka, Traqina Q., and Jon R. Sorensen. "Female Juvenile Risk." *Youth Violence & Juvenile Justice* 7, no. 4 (2009): 313-330
There are few risk assessment instruments that address the unique risk factors for female juvenile offenders. Typically, female risk factors are embedded within male risk factors. Thus, the true differences between male and female juveniles may not be explored. In this study, a generic risk assessment instrument was constructed from a pooled sample and used to identify the level of risk posed by females in comparison with males. Though the constructed instrument worked quite efficiently for males, the instrument provided only a marginal improvement over chance prediction of recidivism for youthful female probationers. Lower rates of predictive validity among the female subpopulation supports call for the development of gendered risk assessment instruments. [ABSTRACT FROM AUTHOR]

Extended Suicide Risk Assessment Form [and] Instruction Manual. Denver, CO: Colorado Division of Youth Corrections, 2011.
The completion of this form is critical in evaluating the potential for juvenile offenders to kill themselves. The form is comprised of eight sections—current problems, present mental state, suicidal issues, intent or potential to harm others, rating of risk, action plan, notification, and documentation.
http://www.colorado.gov/cdhsdyc/P-15-2E.pdf
http://www.colorado.gov/cdhsdyc/P-15-2F.pdf

Fabelo, Tony, Michael D. Thompson, Martha Plotkin, Dottie Carmichael, Miner P. Marchbanks, and Eric A. Booth. Breaking Schools' Rules: A Statewide Study on How School Discipline Relates to Students' Success and Juvenile Justice Involvement. New York: Council of State Governments Justice Center; College Station: Texas A&M University/Public Policy Research Institute, 2011.
This report describes the results of an extraordinary analysis of millions of school and juvenile justice records in Texas. It was conducted to improve policymakers' understanding of who is suspended and expelled from public secondary schools, and the impact of those removals on students'

academic performance and juvenile justice system involvement" (p. ix). Sections following an executive summary include: introduction; overview of the Texas school disciplinary system and key terms; methodology; findings; and conclusion. One of the findings showed that students suspended or expelled for a discretionary violation is almost three times more likely to become involved in the juvenile justice system than students with no disciplinary violations.
http://justicecenter.csg.org/resources/juveniles/report

Fact Sheet: Emerging Findings and Policy Implications from the Pathways to Desistance Study. Washington, DC: National Juvenile Justice Network, 2012.
The Pathways to Desistance study is a large, multi-site, collaborative project that follows over 1,300 youth ages 14-18 for seven years after their convictions. All youth who participated in the study were considered "serious offenders"; many had multiple prior court cases and had just received a conviction for a serious charge—almost exclusively felonies—including murder, robbery, aggravated assault, and sex offenses in either the juvenile or adult system. This fact sheet provides recent findings and policy implications stemming from the research" (p. 1). The four results covered in this publication are: since justice-involved youth are not a homogenous group, predictions regarding future criminal behavior cannot be based on their presenting offense; substance abuse can lead to significant risk for future offending making treatment an important way to reduce recidivism; incarcerating youth does not reduce their chances of re-arrest; and providing a more positive institutional experience for youth results in better outcomes for them. NIC Accession Number: 026778
http://www.njjn.org/uploads/digital-library/Pathways-to-Desistance-Findings-and-Implications9-11-12FINAL.pdf

Fifty State Survey of State Criminal Laws Addressing the Sexual Exploitation of Minors. Washington, DC: NIC/WCL Project on Addressing Prison Rape; American University/Washington School of Law, 2011.
Entries covering the relevant statute(s), age of consent, definitions, defenses, and penalty regarding the sexual exploitation of minors are provided.
http://www.wcl.american.edu/endsilence/documents/FiftyStateSurveyofStateCriminalLawsAdd ressingtheSexualExploitationofMinors2011.pdf
http://nicic.gov/Library/025381

Growing Up LGBT in America: HRC Youth Survey Report Key Findings. Washington, DC: Human Rights Campaign, 2012.

Results from a national survey of lesbian, gay, bisexual, or transgender (LGBT) youth ages 13-17 are presented. "The deck is stacked against young people growing up lesbian, gay, bisexual or transgender in America. Official government discrimination or indifference along with social ostracism leaves many teens disaffected and disconnected in their own homes and neighborhoods. With an increase in public awareness about anti-LGBT bullying and harassment and the strikingly high number of LGBT youth who are homeless, in foster care, or living in high-risk situations, it is critical that we get a better understanding of the experiences, needs, and concerns of LGBT youth." This graphic rich report shows that LGBT youth face a wide range of challenges while also being upbeat and strong.

http://www.hrc.org/files/assets/resources/Growing-Up-LGBT-in-America Report.pdf http://nicic.gov/Library/026170

Hanger, JauNae M. "Screening, Assessment, and Treatment: Indiana Addresses Mental Health in Juvenile Detention Centers." *Corrections Today* 7, no. 1 (2008): 36-38.

The Indiana Juvenile Mental Health Screening, Assessment and Treatment Pilot Project is an innovative, cross-disciplinary effort to establish routine, systematic screening, assessment and treatment in juvenile detention facilities in Indiana. This effort recognizes that a substantial number of youths in the juvenile justice system have unmet mental health needs, and the existing system is largely unable to respond effectively to those needs. Members of the advisory board include legislators; government agencies dealing with child welfare, mental health, education and corrections; juvenile court judges from multiple counties; legal professional associations for probation, juvenile detention, state bar, public defenders and prosecuting attorneys; and medical and mental health representatives - a university adolescent psychologist and one representative from a pediatric physician association, a mental health community centers organization and a minority health coalition.

Hempel, Inge, Nicole Buck, Maaike Cima, and Hjalmar van Marle. "Review of Risk Assessment Instruments for Juvenile Sex Offenders: What is Next?" *International Journal of Offender Therapy & Comparative Criminology* 57, no. 2 (2013): 208-228.

Risk assessment is considered to be a key element in the prevention of recidivism among juvenile sex offenders (JSOs), often by imposing long-term consequences based on that assessment. The authors reviewed the literature on the predictive accuracy of six well-known risk assessment instruments used to appraise risk among JSOs: the Juvenile Sex Offender Assessment Protocol-II (J-SOAP-II), Juvenile Sexual Offence Recidivism Risk Assessment Tool-II (JSORRAT-II), Estimate of Risk of Adolescent Sexual Offence Recidivism (ERASOR), Juvenile Risk Assessment Scale (JRAS), Structured Assessment of Violent Risk in Youth (SAVRY), and Hare Psychopathy Checklist: Youth Version (PCL:YV). Through a systematic search, 19 studies were reviewed. Studies showed differences in the predictive accuracies for general, violent, and sexual recidivism, and none of the instruments showed unequivocal positive results in predicting future offending. Not unexpectedly, the accuracy of the SAVRY and PCL:YV appeared to be weaker for sexual recidivism compared with specialized tools such as the J-SOAP-II or the ERASOR. Because of the rapid development of juveniles, it is questionable to impose long-term restrictions based on a risk assessment only. New challenges in improving risk assessment are discussed. [ABSTRACT FROM PUBLISHER]

Henrichson, Christian, and Valerie Levshin. *Cost-Benefit Analysis of Raising the Age of Juvenile Jurisdiction in North Carolina.* New York: Vera Institute of Justice/Cost-Benefit Analysis Unit, 2011.

Those looking to increase the age of juvenile jurisdiction to 18 will find this report useful in getting their shareholders on board with the change. The North Carolina Youth Accountability Planning Task Force was tasked with "implementing a plan to transfer 16- and 17-year-olds who commit misdemeanor and low-level, non-violent felony offenses to the juvenile system, while keeping 16- and 17-year-olds who commit serious violent felonies in the adult criminal justice system" (p. iii). These sections come after an executive summary: background; cost-benefit methodology; summary of the cost-benefit analysis; costs—law enforcement, courts, juvenile justice operations costs, and juvenile justice capital costs; benefits—criminal justice, victims, and youth; and conclusion. It was determined that the change in age will result in net benefits of $52.3 million a year.

http://www.vera.org/files/cost-benefit-analysis-of-raising-the-age-of-juvenile-jurisdiction-innorth-carolina.pdf

http://nicic.gov/Library/024899

Herz, Denise, Philip Lee, Lorrie Lutz, Macon Stewart, John Tuell, and Janet Wiig. *Addressing the Needs of Multi-System Youth: Strengthening the Connection between Child Welfare and Juvenile Justice.* Washington, DC: Georgetown University/Center for Juvenile Justice Reform; Boston, MA: Robert F. Kennedy Children's Action Corps, 2012.

The purpose of this paper is to provide communities with a consolidated framework for serving crossover youth that incorporates the most up-to-date research, lessons from ongoing reform efforts, and an innovative collaborative management structure" (p. 1). Crossover youth are children involved in both the child welfare and juvenile justice systems. This report is divided into five parts: introduction to dually involved (or crossover) youth and multi-system reform initiatives; understanding the unique experiences of dually-involved youth; the story behind the trends; methodologies addressing the systemic factors impacting dually-involved youth— Systems Integration Initiative (SII) and the Crossover Youth Practice Model (CYPM); and the next frontier and Results-Based Accountability (RBA). The appendix includes a sample resource inventory, sample assessment inventory, and sample maps and flowcharts. http://www.modelsforchange.net/publications/332

Hiscox, Sean P., Philip H. Witt, and Steven J. Haran. "Juvenile Risk Assessment Scale (JRAS): A Predictive Validity Study." *Journal of Psychiatry & Law* 35, no. 4 (2007): 503-539.

A New Jersey Supreme Court decision directed the New Jersey Attorney General's Office to develop a risk assessment scale specific to juvenile sex offenders, to be used to place juvenile sex offenders in risk tiers in accord with New Jersey's community notification law. In light of the court's decision, the scale previously used for both adults and juveniles in New Jersey was modified, creating the JRAS. The present article describes the development of the JRAS. as well as the predictive validity study that was conducted to determine the relationship between JRAS scores and recidivism. The predictive validity study found that the ability of the JRAS to predict both sex offense and non-sex offense recidivism is on the same level as other accepted scales. Factor analysis revealed that the major predictive factor in the JRAS was a general antisocial behavior factor. [ABSTRACT FROM AUTHOR]

Illinois Juvenile Justice Commission Youth Reentry Improvement Report. Chicago: Illinois Juvenile Justice Commission, 2011.

Findings and recommendations for improving the juvenile reentry system in Illinois in order to ensure "safe communities, positive outcomes for our youth, and responsible use of public resources" (p. 9). The proffered strategies for addressing challenges in Illinois' system may help other agencies in addressing short comings in their own juvenile reentry programs. Sections following an executive summary include: methodology; indeterminate sentencing and release decision-making—the current process is inconsistent with Illinois' indeterminate, rehabilitative juvenile justice laws; youth reentry—the current parole system uses an adult surveillance model inconsistent with best practices in juvenile reentry; parole revocation and due process—the current process is not objective and deprives youth of their Constitutional Due Process rights; juvenile justice case management system—the current data system in inadequate for youth tracking, case planning, and monitoring system outcomes.

http://www.dhs.state.il.us/OneNetLibrary/27896/documents/By Division/DCHP/RFP/IJJC Yout hRentryImprovement.pdf

Juvenile Detention in Cook County: Future Directions. Oakland, CA: National Council on Crime and Delinquency, 2011.

Results from an assessment of Cook County's youth detention practices are presented. "This study looks beyond the challenges of the current facility to examine more fundamentally the detention needs of the county and its youth. The ultimate goal of the study is to guide discussion regarding a new vision for detention in Cook County—a vision that holds to the ideals that informed the creation of the court in 1899 while recognizing the current circumstances in which the court operates" (p. 4). Sections following an executive summary include: introduction and background; detention population and practice; program maintenance; physical facility; information systems; and summary recommendations. Appendixes provide information about: the Cook County Screening Form; disproportionate minority contact (DMC) reduction cycle; outline of educational assessment needs; and data-mining experiences. http://nicic.gov/Library/026026

Juvenile Justice Resource Series. Washington, DC: Technical Assistance Partnership for Child and Family Mental Health. Delmar, NY: National Center for Mental Health and Juvenile Justice, 2012.
"This resource series was developed to help communities address the mental health and related needs of young people involved or at risk of involvement with the juvenile justice system ... Each brief examines a unique aspect of serving this population within system of care communities". Papers in the series include: "A Primer for Mental Health Practitioners Working With Youth Involved in the Juvenile Justice System by Robert Kinscherff (2012); "New Directions for Behavioral Health Funding and Implications for Youth Involved in the Juvenile Justice System" by Alison Evans Cuellar (2012); "Screening and Assessment in Juvenile Justice Systems: Identifying Mental Health Needs and Risk of Reoffending" by Gina M. Vincent (2012); "Addressing the Mental Health Needs of Youth in Contact With the Juvenile Justice System in System of Care Communities" by Joseph Cocozza, Kathleen Skowyra, and Jennie Shufelt (2010); "Successfully Collaborating With the Juvenile Justice System: Benefits, Challenges, and Key Strategies" by Shufelt, Cocozza, and Skowyra (2010); and "Systems of Care Programs That Serve Youth Involved With the Juvenile Justice System: Funding and Sustainability" by Skowyra, Cocozza, and Shufelt (2010).
http://www.tapartnership.org/content/juvenileJustice/resourceSeries.php

Latessa, Edward, Brian Lovins, and Kristin Ostrowski. *The Ohio Youth Assessment System: Final Report.* University of Cincinnati, Center for Criminal Justice Research, 2009.
The Ohio Youth Assessment System was designed to assess risk, need, and responsivity factors of youth at each stage of the juvenile justice system. The OYAS provides a composite risk score that is designed to assist juvenile justice actors in making appropriate decisions regarding treatment of youth. [From Summary and Recommendations]
http://www.uc.edu/content/dam/uc/ccjr/docs/reports/projectreports/OYAS finalreport.pdf

Luong, Duyen, and Stephen J. Wormith. "Applying Risk/Need Assessment to Probation Practice and its Impact on the Recidivism of Young Offenders." *Criminal Justice and Behavior* 38, no. 12 (2011): 1177- 1199.
"This study investigated whether risk/need assessment is linked to the case management of young offenders and whether adherence to the principles

of RNR (risk, need, and responsivity), as part of the case management plan, is related to recidivism (p. 1177). Following an abstract, sections of this article include: risk/need assessment, case management, and effective correctional intervention; the Level of Service (LS) Inventory and the LSI-SK (Saskatchewan); the current study; method; results according to the LSI-SK and recidivism and case management (risk and supervision level, needs and interventions—descriptive statistics and appropriateness, responsivity, and prediction of recidivism using risk/need assessment and need-intervention score); and discussion of predictive validity, adherence to risk and need, and limitations and future directions. The LSI-SK has a high degree of predictive validity and high correlation between the LSI-SK total score and recidivism. Accession no. 025516
http://downloads.mhs.com/lscou/Risk-assessment-applied-2011.pdf

Males, Mike. *California Youth Crime Plunges to All-Time Low.* San Francisco, CA: Center on Juvenile and Criminal Justice, 2012.
Reasons contributing to the decrease of juvenile crime in California to its lowest level since 1954, the first year data was collected, are discussed. Sections of this publication include: introduction; California's youth crime decline in detail—California versus the rest of the nation, and charges by race and gender; why California's youth crime has fallen so dramatically—factors that are insignificant to explain the decline (explanations regarding structural changes, demographics, "get tough" policy, family and community, and cultural, and factors that might contribute to the decline (marijuana law reforms, and socioeconomic explanations); and conclusion.
http://www.cjcj.org/files/CAYouthCrime2011.pdf
http://nicic.gov/Library/026777

Mallett, Christopher A., and Patricia Stoddard-Dare. "Predicting Secure Detention Placement for African-American Juvenile Offenders: Addressing the Disproportionate Minority Confinement Problem." *Journal of Ethnicity in Criminal Justice* 8, no. 2 (2010): 91-103.
Disproportionate minority contact and confinement (DMC) are significant problems within the juvenile justice system in the United States. Minority youth are more often arrested, court referred, placed in locked facilities, and transferred to adult criminal courts. In fact, African American youth are 6 times more likely than White youth to experience a secure facility placement. Standardized risk assessments have been used, in part, to

reduce these biased placement outcomes. The purpose of this article is to determine if DMC impacts secure detention placement even when a standardized risk assessment is used to determine youths' risks and needs in one Midwest county's juvenile court population over a 17-month time frame. Multivariate binary logistic regression results indicated and confirmed that African American youth were 2 times more likely to receive secure detention center placement than non-African American youth even when a standardized risk assessment was used. Practical applications and recommendations are set forth. [ABSTRACT FROM AUTHOR]

McGrath, Andrew, and Anthony P. Thompson. "The Relative Predictive Validity of the Static and Dynamic Domain Scores in Risk-Need Assessment of Juvenile Offenders." *Criminal Justice & Behavior* 39, no. 3 (2012): 250-263.

This study examined the predictive validity of the Australian Adaptation of the Youth Level of Service/Case Management Inventory (YLS/CMI-AA). The focus was on the subcomponents of the inventory, which represent one static and seven dynamic risk-need domains. Reoffending outcomes within 1 year of the inventory were obtained for a large sample (N = 3,568) of young people under juvenile justice supervision in the community. Logistic regression analyses investigated the relative contribution of YLS domain scores. The results showed that the static and four dynamic domain scores independently predicted recidivism and that the combination of those domain scores yielded a small improvement in prediction. A similar pattern of results was obtained from analyses of the simple additive scores for the YLS domains. The findings support the YLS/CMI-AA total score as a sufficiently useful predictor of risk, and they clarify the contribution of static and dynamic risk components. [ABSTRACT FROM AUTHOR]

Meyers, Joanna R., and Fred Schmidt. "Predictive Validity of the Structured Assessment for Violence Risk in Youth (SAVRY) With Juvenile Offenders." *Criminal Justice & Behavior* 35, no. 3 (2008): 344-355.

Violence is a serious social problem that is often encountered in the youth justice system. Identifying those adolescents who are at the highest risk for future violence is an important step toward effective rehabilitation. The current study examined the predictive validity of the Structured Assessment for Violence Risk in Youth (SAVRY), a structured professional judgment risk tool, in a sample of 121 juvenile offenders. The SAVRY was found to have strong predictive validity, a finding that was robust across gender and ethnicity. The SAVRY obtained ROC values of .75 and .66 for general and violent recidivism, respectively, for 1 year, and values of .76 and .77 for general and violent recidivism, respectively, for 3-year follow-up. For nonviolent recidivism, the ROC values were .80 for 1-year and .68 during 3 years. Use of the SAVRY in the youth justice system, and limitations of the study, are discussed. [ABSTRACT FROM PUBLISHER]

Ortega Courtney, Katherine, and Jeremy Howard. "Assessing and Improving the Reliability of Risk Instruments: The New Mexico Juvenile Justice Reliability Model." *OJJDP: Journal of Juvenile Justice* 1, no. 1 (2011): 98-106.

Reliability is a critical feature of any screening or assessment instrument; yet, the reliability of juvenile justice risk instruments is rarely assessed. Because their reliability has rarely been examined, we developed a method for examining the reliability of the New Mexico Structured Decision Making Risk Instrument. This method involved creating sample cases that would include information needed to complete the instrument. Two Juvenile Probation Officers (JPOs) from each district in New Mexico were asked to rate ten sample cases. Upon completion of the initial reliability study, we determined that the instrument's reliability was unacceptable. We then undertook an intensive effort to increase its reliability, which included revising definitions and instructions for the instrument and retraining workers statewide. After revising and retraining, we reassessed the instrument's reliability. The results indicated substantial improvement in the instrument's reliability, ensuring equitable application and scoring of risk for youth throughout the state's cultural landscape. The method we used to improve the instrument's reliability resulted in the creation of the New Mexico Juvenile Justice Reliability Model. This method, although new, is relatively simple to use and effective. The resulting model for assessing and improving reliability can be used by others to assess the reliability of their instruments.

http://www.journalofjuvjustice.org/JOJJ0101/JOJJ0101.pdf

Page, Joshua, and Shelly Schaefer. "From Risks to Assets: Toward a Strengths-Based Approach to Juvenile Reentry into the Community." *CURA Reporter* 41, no. 1 (2011): 34-41.

Strategies for making juvenile reentry more effective are described. Such information is vital if a juvenile agency is trying to reform itself into a successful organization. Sections of this article include: probation officer and probationer—a pivotal relationship for the juvenile offender's transition into the community; risk/needs-based versus strengths-based approach; research methodology; case studies; and discussion. A strengths-based approach focuses on juveniles' strengths or assets, provides encouragement and support, fosters empowerment, and collaborates with them on ways to reach their goals.

http://www.jjcmn.com/public/2011/05/Toward-a-Strengths-Based-Approach-to-JuvenileJustice-Reentry.pdf

Penney, Stephanie R., Zina Lee, and Marlene M. Moretti. "Gender Differences in Risk Factors for Violence: An Examination of the Predictive Validity of the Structured Assessment of Violence Risk in Youth." *Aggressive Behavior* 36, no. 6 (2010): 390-404.

The research literature on predicting violence is particularly lacking in specifying risk factors for violence in adolescent girls. The recently developed Structured Assessment of Violence Risk in Youth [SAVRY; Borum et al., 2006] shows promise as it is empirically derived and incorporates dynamic factors in its assessment of risk. To date, there exists little information attesting to the reliability and validity of the SAVRY and few investigations of the SAVRY's utility across gender. This study investigated the SAVRY in a sample of 144 high-risk adolescents (80 males and 64 females), focusing on gender discrepancies in the predictive utility of the measure. Results indicate that the SAVRY moderately predicts violent and non-violent reoffending in the entire sample, and also suggest that the SAVRY operates comparably across gender. Although not precluding the existence of gender-specific domains of risk, current results suggest that validated risk factors in boys hold relevance for the prediction of violence and delinquency in girls.

Perrault, Rachael T., Melissa Paiva-Salisbury, and Gina M. Vincent. "Probation Officers' Perceptions of Youths' Risk of Reoffending and Use of Risk Assessment in Case Management." *Behavioral Sciences & the Law* 30, no. 4 (2012): 487-505.

Juvenile probation officers (JPOs) are required to make numerous decisions about the case management of young offenders on a daily basis. This multi-site study examined JPOs' (N = 64) perceptions of the typical youth's risk of reoffending before implementation of a risk/needs assessment (RNA) tool, and their self-reported, case management decision-making after implementation of an RNA tool. Results indicated that JPOs tended to overestimate the likely base rates of reoffending while RNA tool estimates were more accurate. Further, most JPOs appeared to be making service referral and placement decisions commensurate with youths' risk levels, regardless of whether they claimed to use the RNA tool in their decisions. Variability in application of risk to case management practices was more a function of the probation office than of the specific JPO. Implications for use of risk assessment in juvenile probation are discussed.

Ralston, Christopher A.; Epperson, Douglas L. "Predictive Validity of Adult Risk Assessment Tools With Juveniles Who Offended Sexually." *Psychological Assessment* 2, no. 3 (2013): 905-916.

An often-held assumption in the area of sexual recidivism risk assessment is that different tools should be used for adults and juveniles. This assumption is driven either by the observation that adolescents tend to be in a constant state of flux in the areas of development, education, and social structure or by the fact that the judicial system recognizes that juveniles and adults are different. Though the assumption is plausible, it is largely untested. The present study addressed this issue by scoring 2 adult sexual offender risk assessment tools, the Minnesota Sex Offender Screening Tool-Revised and the Static-99, on an exhaustive sample (N = 636) of juveniles who had sexually offended (JSOs) in Utah. For comparison, 2 tools designed for JSOs were also scored: the Juvenile-Sex Offender Assessment Protocol-II and the Juvenile Risk Assessment Scale. Recidivism data were collected for 2 time periods: before age 18 (sexual, violent, any recidivism) and from age 18 to the year 2004 (sexual). The adult actuarial risk assessment tools predicted all types of juvenile recidivism significantly and at approximately the same level of accuracy as juvenile-specific tools. However, the accuracy of longer term predictions of adult sexual recidivism across all 4 tools was substantially lower than the accuracy achieved in predicting juvenile sexual recidivism, with 2 of the tools producing nonsignificant results, documenting the greater difficulty in making longer term predictions on the basis of adolescent behavior. [ABSTRACT FROM AUTHOR]

Schmidt, Fred, Mary Ann Campbell, and Carolyn Houlding. "Comparative Analyses of the YLS/CMI, SAVRY, and PCL:YV in Adolescent Offenders: A 10-year Follow-Up Into Adulthood." *Youth Violence & Juvenile Justice* 9, no. 1 (2011): 23-42.

A growing body of research has been dedicated to developing adolescent risk assessment instruments, but much of this research has been limited to short-term tests of predictive validity. The current study examined the predictive and incremental validity of the Youth Level of Service/ Case Management Inventory (YLS/CMI), Structured Assessment of Violence Risk in Youth (SAVRY), and Psychopathy Checklist: Youth Version (PCL:YV) in adolescent offenders over a mean 10-year follow-up period. Each instrument predicted general recidivism with moderate- (YLS/CMI area under the curve [AUC] = .66) -to-large effect sizes (SAVRY AUC = .74; PCL:YV AUC = .79). However, there was variation in predictive validity across types of recidivism, and all three instruments were better at predicting recidivism in males than females. SAVRY total also demonstrated incremental validity over its structured professional judgment of risk. Clinical implications and future directions for youth risk assessment are discussed. [ABSTRACT FROM PUBLISHER]

Schwalbe, Craig. "A Meta-Analysis of Juvenile Risk Assessment Instruments: Predictive Validity by Gender." *Criminal Justice and Behavior* 35, no. 11 (2008): 1367-1381.

Juvenile justice systems have widely adopted risk assessment instruments to support judicial and administrative decisions about sanctioning severity and restrictiveness of care. A little explored property of these instruments is the extent to which their predictive validity generalizes across gender. The article reports on a meta-analysis of risk assessment predictive validity with male and female offenders. Nineteen studies encompassing 20 unique samples met inclusion criteria. Findings indicated that predictive validity estimates are equivalent for male and female offenders and are consistent with results of other meta-analyses in the field. The findings also indicate that when gender differences are observed in

individual studies, they provide evidence for gender biases in juvenile justice decision-making and case processing rather than for the ineffectiveness of risk assessment with female offenders.
http://education.ucsb.edu/sharkey/documents/KeyArticle-schwalbe08.pdf

Slobogin, Christopher. "Risk Assessment and Risk Management in Juvenile Justice." *Criminal Justice* 7, no. 4 (2013): 10-25.
The article presents risk assessment and risk management in juvenile justice. Risk assessment is defined as the identification of risk factors and protective factors that influence the involvement in crime. It notes that typical static factors include gender, age and prior criminal history while psychoactive substance use, family support and motivation to alter behavior are among the typical dynamic factors.

Steinhart, David. "Juvenile Detention Risk Assessment." Baltimore, MD: Juvenile Detention Alternatives Initiative. A project of The Annie E. Casey Foundation.
This monograph reviews contemporary juvenile detention risk-screening technology in the United States through the lens of experience provided by JDAI sites. It includes specific recommendations on how to design, test, and implement detention risk-screening instruments. It is written as a practical guide for judges, probation and law enforcement officers, service providers, community leaders, and other juvenile justice decision-makers who are concerned about the quality of care and protection provided to children in the justice system.
In the first part, we examine risk-screening basics—including how risk instrument technology has evolved and has been applied at JDAI sites throughout the nation. In the second part, we present a step-by-step guide to the development, testing, and implementation of juvenile detention risk assessment instruments. In the final part, we address some of the common problems experienced by JDAI sites using new RAIs, and we offer related troubleshooting tips. www.jdaihelpdesk.org

Thompson, Anthony P. and Andrew McGrath. "Subgroup Differences and Implications for Contemporary Risk-Need Assessment with Juvenile Offenders." *Law & Human Behavior* 36, no. 4 (2012): 345-355.
Risk-need assessment is widely accepted as best practice with juvenile offenders and is underpinned by a healthy research literature on risk assessment inventories. Previous studies have found both similarities and

differences on risk measures when gender and racial/ethnic subgroups have been compared. Differential validity has been examined, but differential prediction has been overlooked. The current study undertook gender and ethnic comparisons for a large sample (n = 3568) of community-based juvenile offenders who were evaluated using the Australian Adaptation of the Youth Level of Service/Case Management Inventory (YLS/CMIAA). Analyses showed various gender and ethnic differences at the item level, across domain scores and on the total inventory score, but not for validity indices. However, 1-year reoffending rates for youth in three classification categories (low, moderate, high) varied by gender and ethnicity. The findings were related to contemporary understandings of the risk factors for offending and the dynamics of crime for gender/ethnic subgroups. It is argued that in spite of these subgroup differences, a generic inventory such as the YLS/CMI-AA can be used fairly with various subgroups. Recommendations for how this could be accomplished are provided.

Viljoen, Jodi L., Kaitlyn McLachlan, and Gina M. Vincent. "Assessing Violence Risk and Psychopathy in Juvenile and Adult Offenders: A Survey of Clinical Practices." *Assessment* 17, no. 3 (September 2010): 377-395.

This study surveyed 199 forensic clinicians about the practices that they use in assessing violence risk in juvenile and adult offenders. Results indicated that the use of risk assessment and psychopathy tools was common. Although clinicians reported more routine use of psychopathy measures in adult risk assessments compared with juvenile risks assessments, 79% of clinicians reported using psychopathy measures at least once in a while in juvenile risk assessments. Extremely few clinicians, however, believe that juveniles should be labeled or referred to as psychopaths. Juvenile risk reports were more likely than adult reports to routinely discuss treatment and protective factors, and provide recommendations to reevaluate risk. The implications of these findings are discussed.[ABSTRACT FROM AUTHOR]

Viljoen, Jodi L., Sarah Mordell, and Jennifer L. Beneteau. "Prediction of Adolescent Sexual Reoffending: A Meta-Analysis of the J-SOAP-II, ERASOR, J-SORRAT-II, and Static-99." *Law & Human Behavior* 36, no. 5 (2012): 423-438.

Several risk assessment tools, including the Juvenile Sex Offender Assessment Protocol-II (Prentky & Righthand, 2003), the Estimate of Risk of Adolescent Sexual Offense Recidivism (Worling & Curwen, 2001), the Juvenile Sexual Offense Recidivism Risk Assessment Tool-II (Epperson, Ralston, Fowers, DeWitt, & Gore, 2006), and the Static-99 (Hanson & Thornton, 1999), have been used to assess reoffense risk among adolescents who have committed sexual offenses. Given that research on these tools has yielded somewhat mixed results, we empirically synthesized 33 published and unpublished studies involving 6,196 male adolescents who had committed a sexual offense. We conducted two separate meta-analyses, first with correlations and then with areas under the receiver operating characteristic curve (AUCs). Total scores on each of the tools significantly predicted sexual reoffending, with aggregated correlations ranging from .12 to .20 and aggregated AUC scores ranging from .64 to .67. However, in many cases heterogeneity across studies was moderate to high. There were no significant differences between tools, and although the Static-99 was developed for adults, it achieved similar results as the adolescent tools. Results are compared to other meta-analyses of risk tools used in the area of violence risk assessment and in other fields. [ABSTRACT FROM AUTHOR]

Vincent, Gina M. Screening and Assessment in Juvenile Justice Systems: Identifying Mental Health Needs and Risk of Reoffending. Technical Assistance Partnership for Child and Family Mental Health, 2012.

"This brief will explain why screening and assessment for risk and mental health are best used together by child-serving agencies when planning the most effective course of action for individual youth" (p. 1). Sections of this publication include: how screening and assessment differ; how the above concepts differ for risk assessment tools; how an agency selects a valid tool that is appropriate for its purpose; some examples of tools sued in juvenile justice facilities and community-based services; what the benefits are of screening and assessment are for mental health problems and risk of re-offending; the importance of sound implementation; and conclusion.

http://www.modelsforchange.net/publications/328

Vincent, Gina M., Laura S. Guy, Bernice G. Gershenson, and Patrick McCabe. "Does Risk Assessment Make a Difference? Results of Implementing the SAVRY in Juvenile Probation." *Behavioral Sciences & The Law* 30, no. 4 (2012): 384-405.

An effective approach to reducing recidivism is, first, to identify a youth's risk of reoffending and then to match the intensity of interventions to that risk level. This pre-post quasi-experimental, prospective study compared 247 (pre) with 217 (post) adjudicated youths to examine the implementation of the Structured Assessment of Violence Risk in Youth (SAVRY) and its effects on case management practices in Louisiana's Caddo parish probation office. The results indicated that placement rates dropped by 50%, use of maximum levels of supervision dropped by almost 30%, and use of community services decreased except for high-risk youths, but only after the SAVRY was properly implemented. This shift towards more appropriate allocation of resources that are matched to risk level occurred without a significant increase in reoffending. The implications for implementation and for use of risk/needs assessment in juvenile probation are discussed.

Vincent, Gina M., Laura S. Guy, and Thomas Grisso. *Risk Assessment in Juvenile Justice: A Guidebook for Implementation.* Chicago, IL: Models for Change (MacArthur Foundation), 2012.

The primary purpose of this Guide is to provide a structure for jurisdictions, juvenile probation or centralized statewide agencies striving to implement risk assessment or to improve their current risk assessment practices. Risk assessment in this Guide refers to the practice of using a structured tool that combines information about youth to classify them as being low, moderate or high risk for reoffending or continued delinquent activity, as well as identifying factors that might reduce that risk on an individual basis. The purpose of such risk assessment tools is to help in making decisions about youths' placement and supervision, and creating intervention plans that will reduce their level of risk.

http://modelsforchange.net/publications/346

http://nicic.gov/Library/027092

Vincent, Gina M., Rachael T. Perrault, Laura S. Guy, and Bernice G. Gershenson. "Developmental Issues in Risk Assessment: Implications for Juvenile Justice." *Victims & Offenders* 7, no. 4 (2012): 364-384.

This study investigated two issues in youth risk assessment that may be important to juvenile justice agencies: (1) whether there are age-related differences that might impair the predictive accuracy of risk assessment across adolescence and (2) whether dynamic risk factors provide a unique contribution to risk assessment. The study tracked new petitions over an average 14.5- month follow-up for a large sample (n = 674) of adjudicated young offenders who received the Structured Assessment of Violence Risk for Youth (SAVRY). Findings indicated that age did not moderate the association between the SAVRY and reoffending between youth age 12 and under, age 13 to 15, and age 16 to 18. Dynamic risk factors had incremental predictive validity over static factors for each type of recidivism (e.g., violent, nonviolent) except probation violations. Implications to juvenile justice agencies include the critical importance of including dynamic risk factors in risk assessment tools of youth and the generalizability of these tools across age. [ABSTRACT FROM AUTHOR]

"Webinar: Maximizing the Impact of Juvenile Justice Interventions: The Importance of Risk/Needs Assessment." New York: Council of State Governments. Worcester, MA: Criminal Justice Mental Health Consensus Project, University of Massachusetts Medical School/National Youth Screening and Assessment Project, 2011.

This webinar addresses the use of risk/needs assessment in juvenile justice. It is also a very good introduction to what risk assessment entails. Topics discussed include: what a risk assessment tool is; the national perspective and importance of risk assessment; guiding principles; benefits per dollar invested; valid identification is the first step; ways proper implementation of a risk assessment can save costs; important risk assessment concepts; static risk factors; criminogenic need/dynamic risk factors; elements of a comprehensive risk for re-offending assessment; important developmental concepts; general principles of risk in youth; how to pick an evidence-based risk assessment tool; evidence-based or promising comprehensive risk assessment tools for use post-adjudication; what risk assessments do not do; some points about implementation—risk for re-offending vs. mental health; selection of the risk assessment depends on the decision point in the juvenile justice process; Decision-

Making Model with and without the option of diversion; essential steps of implementation; and the benefits of comprehensive risk assessments. http://www.consensusproject.org/features/webinar-archive-maximizing-the-impact-of-juvenile-justice-interventions-the-importance-of-risk-slash-needs-assessment

ASSESSMENT TOOLS

(Note: This is a partial list; please notify the information team of other tools/systems that should be listed here.)

Child/Family Case Plan (IV-E Residential Placement) [and] Review of Child/Family Case Plan (IV-E Residential Placement). Austin: Texas Juvenile Probation Commission, 2011.
Forms to assist in the development and review of a community supervision plan for a juvenile offender are supplied. "The goals and tasks outlined in this plan are designed to help resolve issues that led to your involvement with the juvenile justice system and to ensure the safety, permanency, and wellbeing of your family" (p. 1). NIC Accession Number: 026542
http://www.tjjd.texas.gov/publications/forms/2004/TJPCFED1204.pdf
http://www.tjjd.texas.gov/publications/forms/2004/TJPCFED1504.pdf

Colorado Juvenile Risk Assessment,
http://www.colorado.gov/cdhsdyc/Resources-Publications/AssessCJRA.pdf

Detention Risk Assessment Instrument (DRAI),
http://www.ocfs.state.ny.us/main/rehab/drai/

Juvenile Risk Assessment Scale,
http://www.nj.gov/oag/dcj/megan/jras-manual-scale-606.pdf

The Missouri Juvenile Risk Assessment Scale,
http://www.courts.mo.gov/page.jsp?id=1200

The Ohio Youth Assessment System,
http://www.uc.edu/content/dam/uc/corrections/docs/OYASOverview2011.pdf

Positive Achievement Change Tool,
http://www.djj.state.fl.us/docs/partners-providers-staff/pactsystem-overview.pdf?sfvrsn=0

Research Support for Evidence-based Practice in Juvenile Justice. Peabody Research Institute/Vanderbilt University, 2011,
http://juvjustice.org/sites/default/files/resource-files/resource 612.pdf

Risk Assessment and Treatment-Focused Instruments Reviewed. Washington, DC: Office of Juvenile Justice and Delinquency Prevention/National Training and Technology Assistance Center,
https://www.nttac.org/index.cfm?event=gsg.WebtoolAlphaListing

Structured Assessment of Violence Risk in Youth (SAVRY),
http://savry.fmhi.usf.edu/

Youth Assessment and Screening Instrument,
http://www.orbispartners.com/assessment/yasi

Youth Level of Service/Case Management Inventory,
http://www.mhs.com/product.aspx?gr=saf&prod=ylscmi&id=overview

JUVENILE JUSTICE: PROGRAMS

Adams, William, and Julie Samuels. *Tribal Youth in the Federal Justice System: Final Report (Revised).* Washington, DC: Urban Institute, 2011. This report looks at issues related to American Indian youth in the federal justice system. Sections following an executive summary are: introduction—overview of the federal justice system, federal jurisdiction involving juveniles, and understanding criminal jurisdiction in Indian Country; exploring current practice—arrest and investigation, prosecution, adjudication and disposition, detention (pre- and post-adjudication), pretrial and post-conviction supervision, and innovative strategies from the field; analysis of federal data; and conclusion. "Tribal and non-tribal juvenile cases differed in significant ways: most tribal youth cases involved violent offenses, while most non-tribal cases involved public order and drug offenses; and tribal youth were more likely to be

adjudicated delinquent, while nontribal youth were more likely to be prosecuted as adults" (p. iii).
http://www.urban.org/uploadedpdf/412369-Tribal-Youth-in-the-Federal-Justice-System.pdf

Askew, Wade, et al. *Kept Out: Barriers to Meaningful Education in the School-to-Prison Pipeline.* Washington, DC: Georgetown Law Human Rights Institute, 2012.
"'Keep Out' is a phenomenon that occurs when students try to reenter a setting where they can access meaningful education and are denied by the policies and practices of the education and juvenile justice systems. Keep Out is a part of the larger School-To-Prison Pipeline. The Pipeline includes disciplinary and discretionary policies that push youth out of school and into the criminal justice system" (p. 7). This report examines the barriers that exist for youth seeking an education following a removal from school. Sections of this report following an executive summary are: introduction; findings about formal and informal policies and practices, lack of coordination and assistance, and failure to educate and support the whole child; conclusion; and recommendations addressing the report's findings.
http://www.law.georgetown.edu/academics/centers-institutes/human-rights-institute/factfinding/upload/KeptOut.pdf

Barton, William H., and Juliette R. Mackin. "Towards a Strength-Based Juvenile Correctional Facility: Sustainability and Effects of an Institutional Transformation." *Journal of Offender Rehabilitation* 51, no. 7 (Oct 2012): 435-452.
In 2006, the administration of a state-run, secure juvenile correctional facility initiated an attempt to transform its institutional culture using a strength-based approach to assessment and case planning. This resulted in a rapid improvement in institutional climate. The current study revisits this setting several years later to see if those improvements were sustained, if they have produced better outcomes for youth, and if the assessment and case planning practices demonstrate fidelity to the intended approach. Results suggest that the institutional climate remains greatly improved and that recidivism results are encouraging, but that implementation of the practice model could be strengthened. [ABSTRACT FROM PUBLISHER]

Bickel, Christopher. "From Child to Captive: Constructing Captivity in a Juvenile Institution." *Western Criminology Review* 11, no. 1 (2010): p37-49.

Juvenile detention centers are not simply places that regulate and control the behavior of children accused of crimes. Nor are they places that "rehabilitate" or "fix" children in need. Instead, juvenile detention centers provide the social location in which detained children, who are often working class and of color, are created unequal, and treated accordingly. I argue that inside juvenile detention centers, children are constructed as "captives," as members of a permanent, disreputable category. Focusing on the experiences of juvenile detention guards, I show how guards construct detained youth as pathological and deserving of punitive treatment. As a result, detained youth are ushered into a rising category of exclusion that carries the salience of other categories of difference, like race, class and gender. "Captivity" is a rising marker of inequality, and is the product of an ongoing interactional process that is reproduced, maintained, and legitimated in the everyday interactions between guards and between guards and detained youth. [ABSTRACT FROM AUTHOR]

Bilchik, Shay; Townsend, Cherie; Davis, Hasan; Hancock, Brain. *Leadership Development: Keys to Leading Juvenile Justice Reform*. National Center for Youth in Custody (NC4YC) (Kalamazoo, MI), 2012.

The role of leadership in fostering change in the juvenile justice system is explained. Topics discussed in this presentation include: introduction—cost savings and matching offender to risk and need; the challenges—collaborative leadership, building a continuum of placements and services, culture change, family engagement, and staff training; measuring outcomes—success defined by reductions in recidivism and other measures of success; juvenile justice reform—the perspectives of the juvenile corrections system; ideal culture; role of leadership; lessons learned; leadership on the line—strategies for engaging frontline youth services staff; show them the R.O.P.E.S. (resources, opportunity, perseverance, expectations, and successes); strengths-based approaches; understanding adolescent development; systems integration; and measure, measure, measure.

http://npjs.org/ncyc/events/event/leadership-

Blevins, Kristie A., Francis T. Cullen, and Jody L. Sundt. "The Correctional Orientation of "Child Savers": Support for Rehabilitation and Custody

Among Juvenile Correctional Workers." *Journal of Offender Rehabilitation* 45, no. 3/4 (2007): 47-83.
Several studies have explored levels and sources of support for rehabilitation and custody among correctional workers. However, the vast majority of this type of research has been conducted in adult facilities, and there are few existing studies that use samples of juvenile correctional workers. To help address this gap in the literature, we use a secondary dataset to examine the levels and sources of correctional orientations among a sample of juvenile correctional workers in Ohio. The results revealed that, like adult correctional workers and the general public, these juvenile correctional workers supported both rehabilitation and custody. An examination of the possible sources of the two orientations indicated that there was a large degree of consensus regarding rehabilitation, while support for custody varied primarily by individual characteristics. [ABSTRACT FROM AUTHOR]

Boulder County Impact: Serving Boulder County's High Risk Youth and Families, http://bouldercountyimpact.org/Home Page.html
Boulder County IMPACT is a multi-agency partnership that was created in 1997 to improve services and systems that work with high-risk children, youth and families. The partnership involves all of the public agencies that serve this target population. IMPACT is part of a statewide initiative that supports a collaborative management model.

Bringing Youth Home: A National Movement to Increase Public Safety, Rehabilitate Youth and Save Money. Washington, DC: National Juvenile Justice Network, 2011.
"This paper includes examples of states that have reduced their juvenile facility populations and are now not only reaping the rewards of new found funds that can be redirected into more effective community-based services for youth, but also seeing a better return on their investment in terms of juvenile rehabilitation and public safety" (p. 1). States highlighted are Alabama, California, the District of Columbia, Florida, Kansas, New York, Ohio, and Texas. Things to consider when downsizing juvenile populations include: treat youth appropriately; reevaluate which youth are being incarcerated; stay focused on disproportionate minority contact; ensure accountability; keep youth in homelike settings; and redirect funds to alternatives to confinement.
http://nicic.gov/Library/025317

Calvin, Elizabeth, Annie Weir, Dana Nahoray, and Austen Breen. *When I Die ... They'll Send Me Home: Youth Sentenced to Life without Parole in California, An Update*. New York: Human Rights Watch, 2012.

This report examines the sentencing of youth in California to life without parole, more or less a death sentence. This text is divided into five parts: youth sentenced to die in California prisons— troubling facts, international norms, adolescent differences from adults, financial costs, and dramatically changing legal perspectives; recommendations; parallel cases, starkly different results; changed lives; and arbitrary outcomes— plea bargaining with a teen, teens perception of time, predicting who a teenager will be at age 40, other existing sentencing law, and changes in California law reducing checks and balances.

http://www.hrw.org/reports/2012/03/01/when-i-die-they-ll-send-me-home-0

The Center for Evidence-Based Mentoring. University of Massachusetts Boston, 2012.

The idea of mentoring youth in correctional facilities may be foreign to some people, yet this strategy for reducing recidivism is a worthwhile choice for your consideration. "The Center is dedicated to creating the open and efficient exchange of research and ideas for the advancement of youth mentoring practice and policy." Points of access to this website are: what's new; about the Center; current projects; Center partnerships; mentoring tools— mentoring support tools, mentoring resources, and related research tools; support and sponsorship; contact information; directions; and The Chronicle of Evidence-Based Mentoring. NIC Accession Number: 026684

http://www.umbmentoring.org/new/index.html

Butts, Jeffrey A., and Douglas N. Evans. *Resolution, Reinvestment, and Realignment: Three Strategies for Changing Juvenile Justice*. New York: John Jay College of Criminal Justice, Research and Evaluation Center, 2011.

Innovative strategies exist for cutting correctional costs by removing juveniles from incarceration in state facilities and placing them under community supervision. "This report reviews the history and development of these strategies and analyzes their impact on policy, practice, and public safety" (p. ii). Reform initiatives are generally of three types: resolution— "direct managerial influence over system behavior"; reinvestment—

"financial incentives to change system behavior"; and realignment—"organizational and structural modifications to alter system behavior." While all three can be effective, realignment appears to be the best strategy for long term sustainability.
http://johnjayresearch.org/rec20111/

Center on Juvenile and Criminal Justice. *Juvenile Placement Manual*. San Francisco, CA: Sentencing Service Program, 2012.
This guide "was developed in an effort to assist juvenile justice practitioners in locating and accessing residential placements for youths in the juvenile justice system. The programs listed are recognized for their ability to address the special needs of youths with extensive histories of juvenile justice involvement." (p. ii). Programs are specific to the placing of juveniles in California and some other states, but information about the programs can be used to implement your own agency's response to the placement of its own juvenile offenders. Each entry includes data (if available) regarding the name of program, address, web site, and specific program information (gender, age, youth accepted, services offered, average length of program, county served, RCL (Rate Classification Level), program type, bed space, visits, after care programs, and additional information).

Cohen, Edward, and Jane Pfeifer. "Mental Health Services for Incarcerated Youth: Report from a Statewide Survey." *Juvenile & Family Court Journal* 62, no. 2 (Mar 2011): 22-34.
The need for mental health care has been steadily increasing for youth coming into contact with the juvenile probation system. This paper presents the results of a statewide survey of juvenile probation departments and associated mental health, health care, court, and education personnel in California. The intent of the survey was to better understand the costs and associated contexts of caring for youth with suspected mental disorders in juvenile detention facilities. The burden of caring for these youth on detention facilities and their staffs is substantial. Implications for courts, policy planning, training, and further research are discussed. [ABSTRACT FROM AUTHOR]

Cooper, Shaun, et al. "Recidivism, Costs, and Psychosocial Outcomes for a Post-Arrest Juvenile Diversion Program." *Journal of Offender Rehabilitation* 50, no. 7 (October 2011): 447-465.

Recidivism, costs, and psychosocial outcomes are reported for a post-arrest diversion program in Wayne County (Detroit), MI. Program features included: rapid, standardized assessment of psychosocial functioning with the Juvenile Inventory For Functioning®, an individualized plan for addressing needs, engagement of caregivers, service provision by youth assistance programs in the youth's community, and access to mental health and substance use services as needed. The adjudication rate for new offenses one-year post services was 7.7%, for a program that costs $1,500 per youth. Significant improvement in functioning was observed for youth with an exit assessment. Functioning at entry predicted recidivism.

Cowell, Alexander J., Pamela K. Lattimore, and Christopher P. Krebs. "A Cost-Benefit Study of Breaking the Cycle Program for Juveniles." *Journal of Research in Crime & Delinquency* 47, no. 2 (May 2010): 241- 262.

The authors present a cost-benefit analysis of a Juvenile Breaking the Cycle (JBTC) program in Oregon designed to provide juvenile justice system monitoring and coordinated treatment and services to youth who are assessed as at high risk for recidivism and substance use. Detailed cost analyses are presented for youth in the JBTC program and a comparison group. Multivariate models for all costs combined indicate that the costs per JBTC youth are much higher than for the comparison group 6 to 12 months after intake. Twelve to 18 months after intake, the difference in juvenile justice costs between the two groups is negligible. These findings suggest that decision makers should not expect any additional case management and treatment costs to be offset immediately by reductions in juvenile justice costs. However, evidence suggests that juvenile justice costs may eventually be at least equivalent to usual care.

Crowe, Ann H., Tracy G. Mullins, Kimberly A. Cobb, and Nathan C. Lowe. *Underage Drinking: Practice Guidelines for Community Corrections.* Washington, DC: U.S. Department of Justice/Office of Juvenile Justice and Delinquency Prevention, 2012.

"In this bulletin, the authors describe 10 guidelines for community supervision professionals who regularly work with underage drinkers. These guidelines are derived from evidence-based practices. They help professionals develop a plan for screening underage drinkers, determine appropriate responses, create a case plan, and provide treatment" (p. 1). These guidelines are: conduct screening for alcohol problems at first and subsequent contacts between underage drinkers and the justice system; assess the youth's risk and need; assess youth for strengths and assets; assess youth for substance abuse problems; determine the most appropriate system-level response and individual-level intervention(s) and develop an individualized case plan; identify each offender's readiness to change and prompt him or her to make positive changes using motivational interviewing techniques; refer underage drinking offenders with alcohol disorders to appropriate alcohol treatment and monitor their attendance and participation; engage family and social support networks in the supervision process; monitor compliance with supervision conditions and case plan expectations; and apply sanctions for noncompliance when necessary, and increase positive reinforcement. http://www.ojjdp.gov/pubs/237231.pdf

Cunningham, James, and Terry Hood. "Keeping the Care in Secure Care." *Reclaiming Children & Youth* 20, no. 3 (2011): 36-40.
The article offers the authors' insights on the management and expansion of the youth assessment and detention services at Starr Commonwealth in Albion, Michigan. They say that the program had two residential areas in which one provided short-term youth detention in Detroit, Michigan while the other area served as a temporary relief for needy Starr Commonwealth residents. They say that as program managers, they have daily contact with new children for their first days. They tackle on the positive response of the youth, the initial communication with parents, and the regular occurrence of informal group meetings. They also mention several positive youth developments including mastery, independence, and generosity.

Dembo, Richard, et al. "Evaluation of an Innovative Post-Arrest Diversion Program: 12-Month Recidivism Analysis." *Journal of Offender Rehabilitation* 47, no. 4 (2008): 356-384.
We report the results of an evaluation study of a diversion program, operated by the Miami-Dade County Juvenile Assessment Center in Florida. The Post-Arrest Diversion (PAD) program represents an innovative approach to treatment and intervention within the juvenile justice system that utilizes standardized psychosocial risks and needs assessment to provide individual treatment for first-time, non-violent juvenile offenders. The present study evaluated the effectiveness of the PAD program with regard to one-year follow-up recidivism. The sample

is comprised of 409 youths (255 male; 154 female) who entered PAD between April and June of 2003. Stepwise, Poisson and OLS regression analyses of the effects of socio-demographic characteristics, type of charges leading to program involvement, recidivism risk level, PAD completion, and arrests while in PAD on the number of recidivism arrests and charges were conducted. The findings suggest that successful completion of PAD significantly reduces recidivism. [Author Abstract]
http://firstsearch.oclc.org/WebZ/DARead?key=1050-9674%252820080826%252947%253A4%253C356%253AEOAIPD%253E%26fsapp8-51043-h9psrhlcuaah54%266d382d212d7b33a7f36a304961675d5d923f75faee03af7649e632a1e805e524&sessionid=0&db=ECOFT&format=PDF

Deitch, Michele. *Juveniles in the Adult Criminal Justice System in Texas.* University of Texas at Austin. Lyndon B. Johnson School of Public Affairs, 2011.
"The common assumption is that certified juveniles [juveniles 14 and older who have committed felony offenses and are transferred to the adult criminal justice system] are the "worst of the worst," repeat, violent offenders who are beyond the rehabilitation offered by the juvenile justice system. But is this assumption in fact true? This report examines all available Texas data with respect to certified juveniles and compares them to the population of juveniles who receive determinate sentences and are placed in TYC [the Texas Youth Commission which is part of Texas' juvenile justice system]. It also compares the significant differences in programming and services for the two populations of juvenile offenders" (p. xi). Sections following an executive summary include: introduction; overview; findings according to numbers of adult certification cases vs. juvenile determinate sentence populations, characteristics of the groups, disposition and sentencing outcomes, and placements and programming; discussion; and recommendations. Research shows that certified youth are not "the worst of the worst"—only those committing heinous crimes, for example 17% committing homicide.
http://www.campaignforyouthjustice.org/documents/juvenilestexas--final.pdf

Driessen, Jerome. "Focusing on Juvenile Justice Reform in Minnesota." *Corrections Today* 73, no. 1 (Feb/Mar 2011): 38-42.

7 Juveniles returning to their family and community after placement need aftercare. Because youths are often released to disorganized communities where it is easy to slip back into the habits that resulted in arrest in the first place, any gains made by juvenile offenders in correctional facilities may quickly evaporate following their release.

Doran, Neal, Melinda Hohman, and Igor Koutsenok. "Linking Basic and Advanced Motivational Interviewing Training Outcomes for Juvenile Correctional Staff in California." *Journal of Psychoactive Drugs* 43, S1 (2011): 19-26.

Results from an evaluation of what was learned by juvenile correctional staff over three-day introductory and two-day advanced motivational interviewing (MI) training sessions are supplied. Results are given for VASE-R (Video Assessment of Simulates Encounters-Revised (VASE-R) outcomes, proficiency outcomes, and MI skills across trainings. "MI skills were positively associated with staff education level, and negatively associated with age and time between trainings... Motivation to use MI, belief in its efficacy with youth, job classification, and sex were not related to skill attainment" (p. 19).

Egan, Kevin W. Evaluation of Juvenile Justice Education Programs: What the Numbers Say about Juvenile Recidivism. University of Central Florida, 2009.

Each year more than 100,000 juveniles are incarcerated in residential rehabilitative facilities. As part of their course of treatment, educational services are mandated for these incarcerated youth. Programs serving these individuals must provide adequate and appropriate educational programs for these juveniles. With a growing public concern over juvenile delinquency and recidivism, programs are being held accountable for the effectiveness and quality of the programming they offer. In Florida, juvenile justice programs offering educational services are monitored annually by the Juvenile Justice Education Enhancement Program. These programs receive a Quality Assurance (QA) rating as determined by a review team that spends several days in the program reviewing documentation and interviewing youth and program staff. This study proposes to examine any potential relationship between the rating a program receives and how successful youth are in returning to mainstream society and subsequently school. Linear regression analysis is the main statistical method to answer four research questions designed to examine these potential relationship. A total of 177 Moderate and High Risk programs were included in the study and the QA scores they received over a three year were analyzed. Surprisingly, the research and subsequent analysis shows little relationship between educational program quality and success rates for juveniles exiting incarceration. This result may warrant further study as to the additional factors contributing to a youth's re-involvement in the juvenile justice system.

Fratello, Jennifer, Annie Salsich, and Sara Modulescu. "Juvenile Detention Reform in New York City: Measuring Risk through Research." *Federal Sentencing Reporter* 24, no. 1 (Oct2011): 15-20.

The article discusses the latest developments in the efforts to reform the juvenile justice system in New York City as of October 2011. The Vera Institute of Justice is cooperating with such agencies as the Office of the Criminal Justice Coordinator (CJC), the Department of Probation, and the Department of Juvenile Justice to reform the system. The two-part reform process include the design of an empirically based risk-assessment instrument (RAI).

Henggeler, Scott W., Sonja K. Schoenwald. "Evidence-Based Interventions for Juvenile Offenders and Juvenile Justice Policies that Support Them." *Social Policy Report* 25, no. 1 (2011): 1-28.

In a context where more than 1,000,000 American adolescents are processed by juvenile courts annually and approximately 160,000 are sent to residential placements, this paper examines "what works" and "what doesn't work" in reducing the criminal behavior of juvenile offenders and presents examples of government initiatives that have successfully promoted the adoption, implementation, and sustainability of evidence-based interventions for juvenile offenders. In general, the vast majority of current juvenile justice services has little empirical support or exacerbates antisocial behavior. These include processing by the juvenile justice system (e.g., probation), juvenile transfer laws, surveillance, shock incarceration, and residential placements (e.g., boot camps, group homes, incarceration). On the other hand, several effective treatment programs have been validated in rigorous research. Effective programs address key risk factors (e.g., improving family functioning, decreasing association with deviant peers), are rehabilitative in nature, use behavioral interventions within the youth's natural environment, are well specified, and include intensive support for intervention fidelity. Although only 5%

of eligible high-risk offenders are treated with an evidence-based intervention annually, inroads to the larger scale use of evidence-based treatments have been made in recent years through federal (e.g., Office of Juvenile Justice and Delinquency Prevention, Substance Abuse and Mental Health Services Administration) and state (e.g., Washington, Ohio, Connecticut, Florida) policy initiatives. Based on our experience transporting an evidence-based treatment within the context of these initiatives, recommendations are made to facilitate stakeholder efforts to improve the quality and effectiveness of rehabilitative services available to juvenile offenders.

Henry, Kelli. Mental Health Services for Justice-Involved Youth: A Process and Outcome Evaluation of QUEST Futures. Center for Court Innovation (New York, NY), 2012.

Results from a process and outcome evaluation of QUEST Futures, a demonstration model designed to address the needs of justice-involved youth with mental health needs in Queens, New York. Information from this report can help you in the event you are looking to implement a similar service in your jurisdiction. Chapters following an executive summary include: introduction; methodology; program model; planning; implementation; participant profile; six case studies of assessment, case management, and treatment; and program outcomes. Appendixes include the following items: Child and Adolescent Needs and Strengths (CANS) form; QUEST Futures Logic Model; NYC Juvenile Detention Risk Assessment Instrument (RAI); Consents to Share Confidential Information; Bio-Psycho-Social Assessment. Participants had a re-arrest rate of 20%.

http://www.courtinnovation.org/sites/default/files/documents/MentalHealthServicesYouth. pdf

Howell, James C., and Mark W. Lipsey. "Research-Based Guidelines for Juvenile Justice Programs." *Justice Research and Policy* 14, no. 2 (2012): 17-34.

"Three ways to define evidence-based programs are described, with a focus on a relatively unfamiliar approach—evidence from meta-analysis of evaluation research that supports the effectiveness of many generic types of programs. In contrast to the prevailing model program approach, this approach makes use of evidence that supports the effectiveness of many of the homegrown and local programs that juvenile justice systems use. The findings of a large meta-analysis of hundreds of studies reveal that many of these more generic programs are as effective as comparable model programs" (p. 17). The three ways evidence-based programs can described are by the specific operating procedure of a particular program, brand name protocol program, and generic intervention type. Sections of this article that following this introduction are: meta-analysis of the recidivism effects of interventions with juvenile offenders; factors related to the magnitude of the recidivism effects; best-practice guidelines for generic intervention types; Standard Program Evaluation Protocol (SPEP) for services to juvenile offenders; pilot testing and validation of the SPEP; and conclusion.

Juvenile Diversion Guidebook. Washington, DC: Models for Change Juvenile Diversion Workgroup, 2011.

Anyone wishing to create or improve juvenile diversion operations and programming will find this guidebook an excellent resource. Three parts comprise this publication: introduction; overview of diversion; and steps for developing and improving juvenile diversion programs— purpose, oversight, intake criteria, operation policies, legal protections, and quality. http://www.njjn.org/uploads/digital-library/MfC
Juvenile Diversion Guidebook March2011.pdf

Kethineni, Sesha, and Jeremy Braithwaite. "The Effects of a Cognitive-Behavioral Program for At-Risk Youth: Changes in Attitudes, Social Skills, Family, and Community and Peer Relationships." *Victims & Offenders* 6, no. 1 (2011): 93-116.

The study evaluated the efficacy of a cognitive-behavioral program in assisting juvenile probationers to change their attitudes, improve social skills, develop positive family relationships, and improve community and peer relationships. A total of 86 medium- to high-risk juvenile probationers in the program were compared with a matched sample of 86 youths who did not participate in the program. Results showed that males in the program showed significant improvements in overall attitudes and family relationships compared to their nonprogram counterparts. The results provide support to existing research that cognitive-behavioral programs, when implemented correctly, show positive changes among high-risk youth.

Key Facts: Youth in the Justice System. Campaign for Youth Justice (Washington, DC), 2012.

This publication is a great primer for those people wanting a concise overview of juvenile justice issues. Information is provided for: youth crime; youth in the juvenile justice system—juvenile court process, and juvenile detention and corrections; youth in the adult criminal justice system—housing youth in adult jails and prisons; racial and ethnic disparities; family involvement; and cost effective alternatives. http://www.campaignforyouthjustice.org/documents/KeyYouthCrimeFact.pdf

Kinscherff, Robert. *A Primer for Mental Health Practitioners Working With Youth Involved in the Juvenile Justice System.* Washington, DC: Technical Assistance Partnership for Child and Family Mental Health (TA Partnership), National Center for Mental Health and Juvenile Justice (Delmar, NY), 2012.

"This paper provides an overview for mental health practitioners who provide professional services to youth who are involved with the juvenile justice system .... While primarily intended for mental health professionals working within system of care communities or interested in developing a system of care collaboration in their area, this paper is relevant for any mental health practitioner providing professional services to youth involved or at risk of involvement in the juvenile justice system. It is also relevant for juvenile court and juvenile justice professionals whose work brings them into contact with youth with significant mental health needs" (p. 1). Sections of this publication include: overview; youth with mental health needs in juvenile justice; mental health clinicians and juvenile justice—strangers in a strange land; distinguishing rehabilitation from treatment; the lens of developmental psychology; diagnosis in juvenile justice—challenges and links to misconduct; common diagnoses among youth in the juvenile justice system—anxiety disorders, mood disorders, attention deficit and disruptive behavior disorders, and substance use disorders; trauma—the chimera or "shape shifter" within juvenile justice; prevalence of trauma in juvenile justice; diagnostic and intervention challenges arising from trauma histories; implications for future policy and practice; and summary. http://www.tapartnership.org/docs/jjResourcementalHealthPrimer.pdf

Koball, Heather, et al. *Synthesis of Research and Resources to Support At-Risk Youth.* Washington, DC: U.S. Dept. of Health and Human Services. Administration for Children and Families/ Office of Planning, Research and Evaluation; Princeton, NJ: Mathematica Policy Research, Inc., 2011.
What is known about at-risk youth and programs that improve the well-being of these youth and foster their ability to be self-sufficient are covered. Other agencies can take this information and use it to develop or enhance their own programs for at-risk youth. Sections comprising this report include: introduction; theoretical perspectives and intervention approaches—the risk and resilience perspective, intervention approaches to increase resiliency, the capital development perspective, intervention approaches focused on capital development, and summary and discussion; ACF (Administration for Children and Families) program resources and existing youth-serving models; and implications for conceptual frameworks—antecedents of adult self-sufficiency among at-risk youth, interventions, linking mechanisms and relative timing for intermediate outcomes and self-sufficiency, long-term adult self-sufficiency, and summary.
http://www.acf.hhs.gov/programs/opre/fys/youthdevelopment/reports/synthesisyouth.pdf

Levin, Marc A., and Bart Lubow. "Juvenile Rehabilitation Versus Incarceration." *Corrections Today* (Jun2012): 10-12.
The article looks at alternatives to incarceration for juvenile offenders in the U.S. It reports that as of 2012, many states have begun to reverse the trend of increasing juvenile incarceration rates. The author discusses evidence that detention of juvenile delinquents is expensive and often counterproductive, compared to community-based programs. He summarizes a 2011 study by the Annie E. Casey Foundation titled "No Place for Kids: The Case for Reducing Juvenile Incarceration."

Lipsey, Mark W., James C. Howell, Marion R. Kelly, Gabrielle Chapman, and Darin Carver. Improving the Effectiveness of Juvenile Justice Programs A New Perspective on Evidence-Based Practice. 2010.
Over the past several years, much attention has been given to evidence-based practice as a way to reduce recidivism rates and improve outcomes for juvenile justice involved youth. Resources such as the Blueprints for Violence Prevention and other similar collections of effective programs have shown the juvenile justice field which programs have been effective

in producing positive outcomes for youth. While this knowledge has greatly benefited the field, little progress has been made in taking evidence-based programs to scale. The apparent gulf between research and practice begs for an innovative solution. While our knowledge of effective programs and practices is significant, the "name brand" programs are often costly, of limited range for the spectrum of services needed or thought to be overvalued when compared to local programs that are anecdotally viewed as effective but lack the resources to show evidence of positive results. Moreover, when evidence-based practices are implemented, they are often operated in silos with the benefit of research-informed practice accruing only to those placed in that particular program. http://cjjr.georgetown.edu/pdfs/ebp/ebppaper.pdf

Loughran, Thomas A., et al. "Estimating a Dose-Response Relationship between Length of Stay and Future Recidivism in Serious Juvenile Offenders." *Criminology* 47, no. 3 (August 2009): 699-740.

The effect of sanctions on subsequent criminal activity is of central theoretical importance in criminology. A key question for juvenile justice policy is the degree to which serious juvenile offenders respond to sanctions and/or treatment administered by the juvenile court. The policy question germane to this debate is finding the level of confinement within the juvenile justice system that maximizes the public safety and therapeutic benefits of institutional confinement. Unfortunately, research on this issue has been limited with regard to serious juvenile offenders. We use longitudinal data from a large sample of serious juvenile offenders from two large cities to 1) estimate a causal treatment effect of institutional placement, as opposed to probation, on future rate of rearrest and 2) investigate the existence of a marginal effect (i.e., benefit) for longer length of stay once the institutional placement decision had been made. We accomplish the latter by determining a dose-response relationship between the length of stay and future rates of rearrest and self-reported offending. The results suggest that an overall null effect of placement exists on future rates of rearrest or self-reported offending for serious juvenile offenders. We also find that, for the group placed out of the community, it is apparent that little or no marginal benefit exists for longer lengths of stay. Theoretical, empirical, and policy issues are outlined. [ABSTRACT FROM AUTHOR]

Macomber, Donna, Thomas Skiba, Jaime Blackmon, Elisa Esposito, Lesley Hart, Elisa Mambrino, Richie Thompson, and Elena L. Grigorenko. "Education in Juvenile Detention Facilities in the State of Connecticut: A Glance at the System." *Journal of Correctional Education* 61, no. 3 (2010): 223-261.

The state of Connecticut detained 1,444 children and youth and committed approximately 270 to the Department of Children and Families for out of home placement in the 2007-2008 calendar year. A significant number of children and youth have special education needs that are often unidentified by home school districts. State and federal law mandate the provision of special education and related services to this population. In addition, education of these individuals is imperative as research indicates educational success is a key component for decreasing recidivism (relapse into unlawful activity) rates and providing opportunities toward productive adulthood. The cost of recidivism to detention is not only monetary; criminal misconduct also threatens the safety of society members as well. The Yale University Child Study Center under the auspices of the Connecticut Judicial Branch, Court Support Services Division (CSSD) conducted a situational analysis of the juvenile detention centers and community residential centers. The focus of this analysis was to: (1) describe the educational characteristics of detained children and youth; (2) describe the educational programs currently used in detention and assess whether the educational programming provided is consistent with the framework of the State of Connecticut Department of Education; (3) typify the community of teachers working with students in detention, identify systemic obstacles and/or challenges to educating this population, ascertain the pathways of educational records of detained children and youth; and (4) identify system barriers or challenges to delivering education to this population and teaching in detention or alternative to detention settings. This report is a summary of findings. [ABSTRACT FROM AUTHOR]

Mallett, Christopher A. "An At-Risk Profile of Probation Supervised Youthful Offenders in a Rural, Midwest County: Significant Gender and Race Differences." *Juvenile & Family Court Journal* 61, no. 3 (Jun2010): 1-12.

There have been multiple risk factors identified that lead to youth delinquent behaviors and activities. These risks are family, school, peer, disability, and neighborhood related, though the studies to date have primarily focused on larger urban juvenile court jurisdictions. This exploratory study of one rural juvenile court (in Ashtabula County, Ohio) furthers these risk factor investigations through the evaluation of 91 randomly selected, adjudicated delinquent youth (supervised in 2008 and 2009). Data on 23 risk factors was collected, with further analysis of significant gender and race differences. Key results were that a majority of youth experienced poverty and lived in a one-parent family; 40% had a mental health or substance abuse problem; 25% were in need of special education disability services; males were much more likely to have school-related difficulties and to commit felony offenses; females had significantly more mental health and substance abuse problems; and minority youth successfully completed probation more often.

Mathur, Sarup R., Heather Griller Clark, and Naomi A. Schoenfeld. "Professional Development: A Capacity-Building Model for Juvenile Correctional Education Systems." *Journal of Correctional Education* 60, no. 2 (June 2009): 164-185.

Youth in correctional facilities experience a broad range of educational, psychological, medical, and social needs. Professional development, a systemic process that improves the likelihood of student success by enhancing educator abilities, is a powerful way to positively affect student outcomes in correctional settings. This article offers a professional development framework designed for the juvenile justice system. It includes information on the background and purpose of professional development, and provides the structure, objectives and components necessary to achieve a capacity-building professional development model in correctional education settings. In addition, examples of the National Center on Education, Disability, and Juvenile Justice (EDJJ) professional development activities, including piloting of professional development modules in a site are discussed. The article concludes with recommendations for future applications of the proposed framework.

Matthews, Betsy; Hubbard, Dana. "The Helping Alliance in Juvenile Probation: The Missing Element in the 'What Works' Literature." *Journal of Offender Rehabilitation* 45, no. 1/2 (2007): 105-122.

Sufficient evidence suggests that building a helping alliance with youth is a viable strategy for addressing treatment needs and reducing delinquency. Strategies recommended in the development of strong helping alliances between youth and probation officers include hiring people with the right values and skills, training staff on the interpersonal skills needed to

develop strong therapeutic relationships, matching staff and youth based on personality characteristics, interests, and skills, assessing staff's capacity to develop strong therapeutic relationships, and supporting staff in their work. Further exploration is needed to gain more knowledge about the importance of building strong relationships with youth in order to challenge the current culture of many modern day probation agencies and deliver effective probation services. Over the past 20 years, much has been learned about the elements of effective correctional interventions through a body of literature known as "what works." The primary foci within this literature are assessment, treatment models, and treatment setting. Relatively little is said about the specific knowledge, attitudes, and skill sets that correctional staff should possess to be effective change agents, or about the importance of the relationships that form between correctional staff and the offenders they serve. The purpose of this paper is to examine the role of the helping alliance in juvenile probation settings. Strategies for facilitating the development of the helping alliance and suggestions for future research are discussed.
https://www.ncjrs.gov/App/publications/abstract.aspx?ID=243580

Mayfield, Jim. *Multisystemic Therapy Outcomes in an Evidence-Based Practice Pilot*. Olympia: Washington State Institute for Public Policy, 2011.
The Multisystemic Therapy (MST) pilot program, "an intensive family- and community-based intervention for chronic juvenile offenders and youth with serious emotional disorders, 12 to 17 years of age, is evaluated (p. 1). Sections of this report include: executive summary; introduction; the intervention and referral process; characteristics of enrolled youth; outcomes regarding subsequent involvement in criminal justice at 12 months and use of public mental health services; summary; and statistical appendix. Participating youth in the MST program are convicted of fewer crimes than non-participants while reducing related costs.
http://www.wsipp.wa.gov/rptfiles/11-04-3901.pdf

McGrath, Andrew, and Don Weatherburn. "The Effect of Custodial Penalties on Juvenile Reoffending." *Australian & New Zealand Journal of Criminology* 45, no. 1 (2012): 26-44.
This study uses propensity score matching to test the proposition that imprisonment deters future criminal activity among juvenile offenders. Using data from all court appearances of juveniles in the NSW Children's

Court (Australia) between 2003 and 2004 (N = 6196), the reoffending of a group of young offenders sentenced to control (i.e. custodial) orders (N = 376) was compared to a matched group of offenders receiving community-based sanctions. No differences were observed between the two groups. The young offenders given detention orders had a slightly lower rate of reoffending, but this difference was not significant. The results of this study indicate that, over the time period examined in this study, the imposition of a custodial sentence had no effect on the risk of reoffending. [ABSTRACT FROM PUBLISHER]

Mendel, Richard A. The Missouri Model: Reinventing the Practice of Rehabilitating Youthful Offenders. Baltimore, MD: Annie E. Casey Foundation, 2012.
States looking to reform their juvenile justice systems will find great strategies within this publication. Sections of this report look at: a better approach to juvenile corrections; nuts and bolts of the Missouri Model—small and non-prisonlike facilities close to home, individual care within a group treatment model, safety through relationships and supervision not correctional coercion, building skills for success, families as partners, and aftercare focus; underlying values, beliefs, and treatment philosophy; organizational essentials; and conclusion.
http://www.aecf.org/~/media/Pubs/Initiatives/Juvenile%20Detention%20 Alternatives%20Initiat ive/MOModel/MO Fullreport webfinal.pdf

Mincey, Barrett, Nancy Maldonado, Candace H. Lacey, and Steve D. Thompson. "Perceptions of Successful Graduates of Juvenile Residential Programs: Reflections and Suggestions for Success." *Journal of Correctional Education* 59, no. 1 (Mar 2008): 8-31.
Abstract: This qualitative study conducted in urban Miami, Florida, explored the essence of juvenile delinquency and recidivism: its causes, its relations to communities, the roles of families, and the myriad roles of residential treatment programs at rehabilitating young offenders. Data were collected from nine young adult participants who had satisfied their court-ordered sanctions in different residential facilities. Data were analyzed to discover themes, patterns, or clusters of meanings. Several themes and sub-themes emerged. These included overcoming patterns of delinquent behaviors, facing challenges of remaining focused and goal-oriented, and providing suggestions for young offenders as well as recommendations for change to correctional leaders and accounts of

successes and failures. Implications are included for lawmakers, criminologists, and juvenile justice administrators as measures for reducing juvenile delinquency and recidivism. [PUBLICATION ABSTRACT]

Models for Change: Systems Reform in Juvenile Justice. Washington, DC: Models for Change. Sponsored by John D. and Catherine T. MacArthur Foundation (Chicago, IL), 2012.

"Models for Change collaborates with selected states to advance juvenile justice reforms that effectively hold young people accountable for their actions, provide for their rehabilitation, protect them from harm, increase their life chances, and manage the risk they pose to themselves and to public safety." This website provides access to: issues for change—leverage points to stimulate reforms; states for change—states selected for their strategic leadership; action networks—collaboration between state and local partners; reform progress; calendar; National Resource Bank; publications; newsroom; and about Models for Change. http://www.modelsforchange.net/index.html

Moll, Jeanette. *Ten Truths about Juvenile Justice Reform.* Austin: Texas Public Policy Foundation, Center for Effective Justice, 2011.

Guidance on how to achieve reductions in operational expenditures while implementing comprehensive juvenile justice reform is provided. While this publication is targeted for state lawmakers, its content should be taken into account by local decision makers. state Reform efforts should incorporate the following ten truths about juvenile justice: confinement is still necessary; juvenile residential programs should be community-based when possible; confinement should not be the default response; risk and needs assessments are important; traditional forms of discipline by parents and schools are still best; probation is an existing viable alternative; juveniles, even if sentenced as adults, should not go directly into adult facilities; performance incentive funding (PIF) increases productivity, cost-efficiency, and positive outcomes; and reform is possible. http://www.texaspolicy.com/pdf/2011-12-PP21-TenTruthsAboutJuvenileJusticeJeanetteMoll.pdf

Morris, Richard J; Thompson, Kristin C. "Juvenile Delinquency and Special Education Laws: Policy Implementation Issues and Directions for Future

Research." *Journal of Correctional Education* 59, no. 2 (Jun 2008): 173-190.

The research literature has repeatedly demonstrated that there is an overrepresentation of juveniles with disabilities who are incarcerated in short-term and long-term correctional facilities. Despite these findings, special education programs in many juvenile correctional facilities have been shown to be lacking many of the necessary services mandated by federal law. The present article discusses the various legal challenges and difficulties faced by juvenile correctional education programs in providing special education services to incarcerated juveniles with disabilities, as well as the legislation and case law that currently exist to protect the right to special education services for all eligible juveniles. Related policy implementation issues and suggestions for future research in this area are also discussed. [PUBLICATION ABSTRACT]

Muller, Eve. *Reentry Programs for Students with Disabilities in the Juvenile Justice System: Four State Approaches*. Project Forum; National Association of State Directors of Special Education (NASDSE). Sponsored by U.S. Dept. of Education. Office of Special Education Programs, 2011.

"Evidence strongly supports the notion that juvenile offenders, both with and without disabilities, are significantly more likely to experience successful reentry into their home schools and communities if appropriate programs and supports are in place" (p. 1). Strategies for effectively meeting the reentry needs of disabled justice-involved youth are described. Sections of this analysis include: overview and background—what reentry is, federal efforts to support successful reentry, prevalence of students with disabilities I the juvenile justice system, why reentry programming matters, and recommended reentry strategies; examples of state reentry approaches and common themes for Arizona, Georgia, Hawaii, and Oregon. http://nasdse.org/DesktopModules/DNNspot-Store/ProductFiles/660082f096-5a9d-49f7-a2c1- c6ff737af209.pdf http://nicic.gov/Library/025837

Mulvey, Edward P. *Highlights From Pathways to Desistance: A Longitudinal Study of Serious Adolescent Offenders*. Washington, DC: U.S. Department of Justice, Office of Juvenile Justice and Delinquency Prevention, 2011.

Findings are presented from the Pathways to Desistance Study, the most comprehensive and current data set for serious adolescent offenders.

Individuals working with justice-involved youth should be familiar with this summary. Major observations include: regardless of interventions utilized, most youth who commit felonies greatly reduce their offending over time; longer stays in juvenile institutions do not reduce recidivism; the use of community-based supervision as part of aftercare is effective for youth who have committed serious offenses; and substance abuse treatment reduces both substance use and criminal offending. http://ncjrs.gov/pdffiles1/ojjdp/230971.pdf
http://nicic.gov/Library/024956

National Conference of State Legislatures. *Trends in Juvenile Justice State Legislation: 2001-2011.* Denver, CO: National Conference of State Legislatures, 2012.
"States are re-evaluating their juvenile justice systems in order to identify methods that produce better results for kids at lower cost. This has contributed to a state legislative trend to realign fiscal resources from state institutions toward more effective community-based services" (p. 3). Sections following an executive summary discuss: distinguishing juvenile offenders from adults—adolescent developmental research, federal standards, raising the age of juvenile court jurisdiction, reforming transfer and direct file laws, and juvenile competency; landmark juvenile life without parole decision—Miller v. Alabama (2012); due process and procedural issues—legal counsel and other procedural issues, and indigent defense; prevention and intervention— evidence-based programs, and diversion and investing in community-based alternatives to incarceration; treating mental health needs of juvenile offenders—screening and assessment; highlights of other significant juvenile mental health laws; disproportionate minority contact; detention and corrections reform; reentry/aftercare- confidentiality of juvenile records and expungement; gender-responsive programming; and conclusion.
http://www.ncsl.org/issues

National Juvenile Justice Network. *Senate Bill No. 9: California Fair Sentencing for Youth Act.* Sacramento: California State Assembly, 2012.
"An act to amend Section 1170 of the Penal Code, relating to sentencing ... This bill would authorize a prisoner who was under 18 years of age at the time of committing an offense for which the prisoner was sentenced to life without parole to submit a petition for recall and resentencing to the sentencing court, and to the prosecuting agency, as specified. The bill

would prohibit a prisoner who tortured his or her victim or whose victim was a public safety official, as defined, from filing a petition for recall and resentencing. The bill would require the petition to include a statement from the defendant that includes, among other things, his or her remorse and work towards rehabilitation. The bill would establish certain criteria, at least one of which shall be asserted in the petition, to be considered when a court decides whether to conduct a hearing on the petition for recall and resentencing and additional criteria to be considered by the court when deciding whether to grant the petition. The bill would require the court to hold a hearing if the court finds that the statements in the defendant's petition are true, as specified. The bill would apply retroactively, as specified" (p. 92). http://www.njjn.org/uploads/digital-library/California-Fair-Sentencing-for-Youth-Act-CA-SB9 bill 20120821 enrolled.pdf?utmsource=Victory+in+California&utmcampaign= Newsletter% 3A+Oct+5%2C+2012&utm medium=email

National Juvenile Justice Network. The Truth about Consequences: Studies Point toward Sparing Use of Formal Juvenile Justice System Processing and Incarceration. Washington, DC, National Juvenile Justice Network, 2012.
"Recent research on the juvenile justice system indicates that in nearly all instances, the best public safety outcomes coincide with the least restrictive interventions for youth, rather than more traditional processing and intervention ... costly incarceration of youth contrasts sharply with diversion programs and community-based alternatives, which, when done right, cost less and reduce recidivism" (p. 1). The noted studies show that formal system processing does not reduce delinquency and that incarceration is ineffective. http://www.njjn.org/our-work/juvenile-justice-system-incarceration-the-truth-about-consequences-

National Juvenile Justice Network. *Using Adolescent Brain Research to Inform Policy: A Guide for Juvenile Justice Advocates.* Washington, DC: National Juvenile Justice Network, 2012.
This paper is an excellent overview of the dramatic impact that changes in their brains have on their behavior. Anyone working with juveniles should know about brain research. Sections of this fact sheet include: introduction; what the research says; how this affects young people's behavior; it is not too early to use this research; how to respectfully frame the research; how brain research relates to positive youth development;

one caution—brain development research can be negatively applied; and conclusion.
http://www.njjn.org/our-work/adolescent-brain-research-inform-policy-guide-for-juvenilejustice?utmsource=Victory+in+California&utm campaign=Newsletter%3A+Oct+5%2C+2012&u tmmedium=email

Neelum, Arya. State Trends: Legislative Victories from 2005 to 2010 Removing Youth from the Adult Criminal Justice System. Washington, DC: Campaign for Youth Justice, 2011.
Reforms that return youth back to juvenile courts, actions supported by public opinion and cost savings, are described. States looking to cut budget deficits will find useful strategies for dealing with these fiscal difficulties. Sections of this report include: how a youth ends up in the adult justice system; overview; understanding the consequences of trying youth as adults—teen brains are not fully developed, most youth are convicted of minor crimes, they are housed in adult facilities, such prosecution leads to more crime, youth face lifelong barriers to employment, and disproportionate impacts on youth of color; four trends to watch—removal of youth from adult courts and facilities, age of juvenile court jurisdiction is raised, transfer laws are changed, and youth sentencing laws are reconsidered; and recommendations for policymakers. "[R]eturning youth to juvenile court jurisdiction will result in a $3 savings benefit for every $1 spent" (p. 4).
http://www.campaignforyouthjustice.org/documents/CFYJStateTrendsReport.pdf

Nellis, Ashley. "Juvenile Justice: Addressing the Collateral Consequences of Convictions for Young Offenders." *The Champion* (July/August 2011): 20-24, 26-27.
"This article explores areas in need of attention and reform so that young people who have been adjudicated delinquent or convicted of a crime are not punished subsequently by other systems they encounter" (p. 20). Topics covered include: an overview of the juvenile offender population; original intent of the juvenile justice system; collateral consequences of a conviction or delinquency adjudication—zero tolerance and other school push-out policies, challenges to re-enrollment, barriers to employment, eviction and homelessness, and placement on a national or state sex offender registry; and conclusion.

http://sentencingproject.org/doc/publications/Collateral%20Consequences %20NACDL%202011. Pdf

Nellis, Ashley. The Lives of Juvenile Lifers: Findings from a National Survey. Washington, DC: The Sentencing Project, 2012.
This report presents data from the first survey about juvenile lifers. This is especially important since the United States is the only country in the world that incarcerates a juvenile (for) life without parole (JLWOP)—meaning this child will die in the prison. Anyone working with incarcerated children especially those for life without parole need to read this publication. Key findings are given for: socioeconomic disadvantages, education failure, and abuse; extreme racial disparities in JLWOP sentences; JLWOP sentences frequently imposed mandatorily; and corrections policies curtail efforts at rehabilitation. Sections following key findings include: a betrayal of American juvenile justice system principles; juvenile lifers—a portrait of disadvantage; dynamics of the crime; life in prison; summary of findings; JLWOP—historical and legal perspectives; impact of JLWOP on individuals and public safety; and recommendations for reform. "Although it does not excuse their crimes, most people sent to prison for life as youth were failed by systems that are intended to protect children" (p. 2).
http://org2.democracyinaction.org/dia/track.jsp?v=2&c=%2Bo6IseGaD% 2F7RzJ7UA0Rz0cQwly UFihXP

"New York City Reduces Reliance on Juvenile Detention--Rearrest Rates Drop." *Criminal Justice Research Review* 13, no. 2 (Nov/Dec 2011): 23-25.
The article discusses the effort of New York City to address the problem on high cost of secure detention through a two-state process. It notes the process including the development and implementation of an empirically based risk-assessment instrument (RAI) and the creation of a community-based, nonresidential programs to provide an alternative to secure detention. It adds that the implementation of RAI has reduced the city's detention use and has improved case outcomes.

Ortiz-Schumeyer, Zulma. "Factors Leading to High Recidivism Rates Among Juvenile Delinquents at Three Correctional Facilities in New York City." Northcentral University, 2008.

The purpose of this study was to examine factors leading to recidivism rates among juvenile delinquents. The researcher collected data from the Department of Juvenile Justice OCFS (ready respondents records of youth adjudicated, released and re-arrested). The researcher reviewed pertinent literature of the factors of recidivism and the programs, procedures, and methodologies that have been implemented throughout the United States to address this problem. In an effort to greater identify factors that lead to recidivism rates in the three Correctional Facilities in New York City, a standardized data collection instrument was established that examined documents in each participant's probation case file. A qualitative and descriptive study approach was utilized. A survey and questionnaire were used to collect data. The findings provide an in-depth description of the characteristics, demographics and other factors that lead to recidivism, implications of why youth continue to come in and out of correctional facilities and recommendations to help prevent future re-offending. One significant factor was a youth's family structure. Connections to school were also related to juveniles' law-violating behavior. Youth who rarely or never attended school had a significantly greater risk of engaging in a wide range of problem behavior such as using marijuana, running away from home, belonging to a gang, committing a major theft or a serious assault, and selling drugs.

Page, Joshua, and Shelly Schaefer. "From Risks to Assets: Toward a Strengths-Based Approach to Juvenile Reentry into the Community." *CURA Reporter* 41, no. 1 (2011): 34-41.

Strategies for making juvenile reentry more effective are described. Such information is vital if a juvenile agency is trying to reform itself into a successful organization. Sections of this article include: probation officer and probationer—a pivotal relationship for the juvenile offender's transition into the community; risk/needs-based versus strengths-based approach; research methodology; case studies; and discussion. A strengths-based approach focuses on juveniles' strengths or assets, provides encouragement and support, fosters empowerment, and collaborates with them on ways to reach their goals.
http://www.jjcmn.com/public/2011/05/Toward-a-Strengths-Based-Approach-to-JuvenileJustice-Reentry.pdf

Pennell, Joan; Shapiro, Carol; Spigner, Carol. *Safety, Fairness, Stability: Repositioning Juvenile Justice and Child Welfare to Engage Families and*

Communities. Georgetown University, Public Policy Institute. Center for Juvenile Justice Reform (CJJR) (Washington, DC), 2011.
The need to strengthen the ties between family members and youth involved in the juvenile justice system is explained. Family engagement is one strategy for agencies working to create "pro-social connections that will support them [juvenile offenders] in their path to adulthood" (p. v). This report is divided into six parts: introduction and background; shifting views of parents and youth—historical development and opportunity for change; family engagement—what it means; practice strategies—putting family into action; process and outcomes—what helps; and repositioning--next steps. Appendixes provide: systems of care values and principles; achievement of family group conferencing objectives; Judicial Relational Inquiry tool; and tools for identifying family and community relationships. http://cjjr.georgetown.edu/pdfs/famengagement/FamilyEngagementPaper.pdf

Peters, Colette S., and Shannon Myrick. "Juvenile Recidivism - Measuring Success or Failure: Is There a Difference?" *Corrections Today* 73, no. 1 (2011): 33-35.
http://www.oregon.gov/oya/docs/correctionstodaymarch2011.pdf

PREA in the Juvenile Justice System Resources. Oregon Youth Authority (Salem, OR) National PREA Resource Workgroup (Salem, OR), 2011.
What makes this webpage unique is its offering of PREA (Prison Rape Elimination Act) material for the juvenile justice setting. Points of access include: publications; useful links; and training materials and samples from Oregon—training presentation, youth safety letters, surveys, youth safety tools and promos, and tracking tool. There are also links to news, discussions, and connections (related organizations nationwide). http://www.oregon.gov/OYA/prea/prearesources.shtml

PREA Training Video: Addressing Sexual Misconduct in the Juvenile Corrections Environment (Full); Indiana Department of Correction PREA Training video. Calamari Productions (Indianapolis, IN) Indiana Dept. of Correction (Indianapolis, IN), 2012.
"Full length training video for educating Juvenile Corrections staff on the sensitive issue of offender sexual misconduct. The video delves into the topics of: understanding juvenile offenders, dealing with juvenile sex offenders, handling offender-on-offender sexual misconduct, preventing

staff-on-offender sexual misconduct, and managing reactions to offender masturbation."
http://vimeo.com/26700677

Puzzanchera, Charles, and Benjamin Adams. *Juvenile Arrests 2009.* Washington, DC: U.S. Dept. of Justice. Office of Juvenile Justice and Delinquency Prevention: 2011.
This publication provides a "comprehensive statistical overview of the problems of juvenile crime, violence, and victimization and the response of the juvenile justice system" (p. 1). Data show that juvenile crime is not on the rise. Arrests of juveniles for violent offenses dropped 10% from 2008 to 2009. Since arrest rates hit their peak in 1994, there has been a decline of almost 50%. Yet, the juvenile arrest rate for simple assault, which is the most common juvenile crime against people, has risen 15% since 1980.
http://ojjdp.gov/publications/PubAbstract.asp?pubi=258483

Rawan Ibrahim, et al. "A Meta-analysis of Experimental Studies of Diversion Programs for Juvenile Offenders." *Clinical Psychology Review* 32, no. 1 (February 2012): 26-33.
Research to establish an evidence-base for the treatment of conduct problems and delinquency in adolescence is well established; however, an evidence-base for interventions with offenders who are diverted from the juvenile justice system has yet to be synthesized. The purpose of this study was to conduct a meta-analysis of experimental studies testing juvenile diversion programs and to examine the moderating effect of program type and implementation quality.

Renewing Juvenile Justice. San Francisco, CA: Center of Juvenile and Criminal Justice San Francisco, CA, 2011.
This report "offers recommendations for policy changes to improve practice in local jurisdictions and expand services for high-risk youthful offenders ... [and] with the expectation that it will be a helpful tool for local jurisdictions and philanthropic partners interested in reshaping and ultimately renewing juvenile justice practice." While the focus of this publication is on California, foundations in other states will find this information useful in the event they plan to partner with local jurisdictions in the systemic reform of their juvenile justice systems. Seven section follow and executive summary with recommendations: historical

overview of juvenile justice in California; the current state of the California juvenile justice system; statistical overview of the 26 counties served by the Sierra Health Foundation; planning for a 21st century juvenile justice system; constructing a model system; implementing reform—fist steps; and conclusion.
http://www.sierrahealth.org/assets/pubs/SHF RJJ Report Final.pdf

Richards, Kelly. *What Makes Juvenile Offenders Different from Adult Offenders?* Canberra, ACT: Australian Institute of Criminology, 2011.
"This paper outlines the factors (biological, psychological and social) that make juvenile offenders different from adult offenders and that necessitate unique responses to juvenile crime" (p. 1). Anyone connected to juveniles involved with the criminal justice system needs to be aware of the findings gleaned from this study. Sections of this publication are: how juvenile offending differs from adult offending—the proportion of crime perpetrated by juveniles, growing out of crime and the age-crime curve, juvenile offending trajectories, the proportion of juveniles who come into contact with the criminal justice system, the types of offences that are perpetrated by juveniles, and the nature of juvenile offending; why juvenile offending differs from adult offending—risk-taking and peer influence, intellectual disability and mental illness, and young people as crime victims; the challenge of responding to juvenile crime—juvenile offenders have complex needs, they require a higher duty of care, and they may grow out of crime; juvenile justice interventions--the doctrine of doli incapax, welfare and justice approaches to juvenile justice, reducing stigmatization, addressing juveniles' criminologic needs, diversion of juveniles, and avoiding peer contagion; and conclusion.
http://www.aic.gov.au/documents/4/2/2/%7B4227C0AD-AD0A-47E6-88AF399535916190%7Dtandi409.pdf

Rodriguez, Nancy. "Juvenile Court Context and Detention Decisions: Reconsidering the Role of Race, Ethnicity, and Community Characteristics in Juvenile Court Processes." *Justice Quarterly* 24, no. 4 (December 2007): 629-656.
Abstract: The relationship between race/ethnicity, community dynamics, and juvenile court processes has long been established. Prior research has relied on city- or county-level measures of community characteristics (e.g., racial composition, poverty) to examine how racial groups are processed within juvenile courts. To date, no study has utilized finer scale

measures of geographic areas to examine how characteristics of juveniles' communities impact court decisions. By utilizing official juvenile court data from a city in the southwest, this study draws upon attribution theory to examine how economic and crime community-level measures directly and indirectly influence detention outcomes. Findings reveal that the effect of race and ethnicity in detention outcomes varies across communities, and the effect of ethnicity in detention decisions is mediated by economic community-level measures. The theoretical and policy implications of the study findings are discussed. [ABSTRACT FROM AUTHOR]

Roush, David W. "Cognitive Behavioral Intervention with Serious and Violent Juvenile Offenders: Some Historical Perspectives." *Federal Probation* 72, no. 3 (Dec 2008): 30-36, 57.

Cognitive Behavioral Intervention (CBI) is an increasingly popular strategy for juvenile justice policy makers and practitioners looking for an effective way to meet public expectations for safety, security, and rehabilitation while addressing the various needs of the juvenile offender population (Glick, 2006a). The juvenile correctional community's desire to define good faith practice in response to these court decisions and the growing body of case law involving juvenile institutions was a motivating factor for the American Correctional Association (ACA) to develop professional standards for juvenile detention and juvenile corrections facilities (Farkas, 1977; Sechrest, 1978), the first editions of which appeared in 1979 (Commission on Accreditation for Corrections, 1979).

Rubin, Ted H. "A Look at the Impact of Distance on Juvenile Justice Practices." *Juvenile Justice Update* 16, no. 2 (Apr/May 2010): 1-12.

The article discusses the impact of distance on a variety of juvenile justice practices and services in court participation and outcomes. It talks about the efficiency of telecommunications in juvenile detention hearings used in many adult jails for bond hearings or arraignments and the importance of the involvement of parents in detention decision. It mentions the role of cultural distances in probation and juvenile court systems.

Rudes, Danielle S., Jill Viglione, and Faye S. Taxman. "Juvenile Probation Officers: How the Perception of Roles Affects Training Experiences for Evidence-Based Practice Implementation." *Federal Probation* 75, no. 3 (2011): 3-10.

The impact on probation officers (POs) when they implement evidence-based practices (EBPs) is examined. This article contains these sections: literature review for probation officer roles and interaction between PO roles and training; method; findings regarding PO roles, view of training, and perception of probationers, and type of training; and discussion. "In summary, findings revealed that role orientation and perceptions of training or probationers are not directly related. In addition, analysis of study group participation displayed only one clear relationship: positive views of both training and probationers resulted from participants in the enhanced training group. Further, perceptions of additional training tools were mixed amongst role orientation and study group participants. These findings have important implications for structuring EBP training and implementing EBPs in probation agencies" (p. 10).
http://www.uscourts.gov/uscourts/FederalCourts/PPS/Fedprob/2011-12/evidence-based.html

Schwalbe, Craig S., and Tina Maschi. "Patterns of Contact and Cooperation between Juvenile Probation Officers and Parents of Youthful Offenders." *Journal of Offender Rehabilitation* 49, no. 6 (Aug/Sep 2010): 398-416.
This study documents patterns of contact between juvenile probation officers and parents and examines factors associated with officer judgments about parental cooperation. Data for the study was derived from a Web-based survey of probation officers (N = 308) who reported their use of probation strategies with specific youths identified from their caseloads. Results showed that parent contacts were predicted by parent and youth drug use, parent and youth cooperation, and officer attitudes favoring punishment. Parental cooperation with probation processes was predicted by youth and parent drug use problems, parent offending history, youth cooperation, and race. Results of this study point to the need for evidence-based strategies to promote parental involvement for high risk and high need families.

Sells, Scott, Irene Sullivan, and Donald Donald. "Stopping the Madness: A New Reentry System for Juvenile Corrections." *Corrections Today* 74, no. 2 (2012): 40-45.
If you are looking for a strategy to reduce the increasing rates of juvenile recidivism in your jurisdiction then this article should be on your "Must Read" list. The promising evidence-based reentry model described herein is called Parenting with Love and Limits (PLL). PLL is being utilized in

seven states. Sections of this article include: one potential solution—a new reentry operating system utilizing community-level collaboration; summary of reentry delivery system changes; five recommendations for successful juvenile systems; and conclusion. “The process of changing reentry is not easy but must happen quickly due to the budget crisis and the fact that states must safely reduce lengths of stay whether they want to or not. The PLL reentry model offers one such solution with a set of unique components that includes a customized delivery system for reentry” (p. xxx).
http://www.aca.org/fileupload/177/ahaidar/SellsSullivan.pdf

Shields, Danielle M. “Warehoused: The Plight of 'Mad' Youths in the Juvenile Justice System.” *Justice Policy Journal* 8, no. 1 (Mar 2011): 48, 36p.
On any given day, tens of thousands of youths are housed in juvenile correctional facilities and unfortunately, a staggering proportion of these individuals suffer from mental illness. Though juvenile justice facilities are largely ill-equipped to serve as surrogate mental institutions, they have assumed this role out of necessity, as there is a distinct lack of community treatment options for mentally ill juveniles. Faced with inadequate assessment and treatment practices once they are absorbed into the correctional system, many incarcerated mentally ill youth are simply warehoused. Drawing upon available research, this paper recounts the historical events that contributed to the current dearth of community treatment options for juveniles, describes the prevalence, treatment, and assessment of mental illness among juvenile detainees, and considers alternatives to the current policies that exist within the system. [ABSTRACT FROM AUTHOR]

Smith, Malcolm L., and Karen Myers Bowman. “The Restraint Spiral: Emergent Themes in the Perceptions of the Physical Restraint of Juveniles.” *Child Welfare* 88, no. 3 (May/Jun2009): 57-83.
This qualitative investigation explores the experiences of both children who were physically restrained in a juvenile facility and that of the adult professionals who restrained them. Among the major themes identified were the rationalizations of safety and noncompliance for restraint use by the adults. Children associated fear, anger, and retraumatization with the experience of being restrained. Both the children who were restrained and the adults who restrained them identified lingering emotional and behavioral postrestraint effects. Restraint incidents were found to follow a

predictable 10-layered behavioral spiral. Implications for practice and further research are explored. [ABSTRACT FROM AUTHOR]

Snow, Pamela, and Martine Powell. "Youth (in)justice: Oral Language Competence in Early Life and Risk for Engagement in Antisocial Behaviour in Adolescence." *Trends & Issues in Crime and Criminal Justice* no. 435 (April 2012).

"This paper is concerned with the growing body of evidence, both in Australia ... and overseas that identifies oral language competence as a key competency that needs to be acquired early in life, so that important interpersonal, academic and vocational goals can be achieved in pro-social ways and the risk of offending behaviour can be reduced" (p. 1). Sections of this publication cover: what oral language competence is and why it matters; what the literature tells us about early psycho-social risk and language development; the international literature on the language skills of young offenders; implications related to early identification of high-risk boys, interventions within juvenile justice, forensic interviewing, and Restorative Justice Conferencing (RJC); and the future.

http://www.aic.gov.au/publications/current%20series/tandi/421-440/tandi435.aspx

Steinberg, Laurence. "Should the Science of Adolescent Brain Development Inform Public Policy?" *The American Psychologist* 64, no. 8 (Nov 2009): 739-750.

One factor that has contributed to confusion in discussions of the use of adolescent neuroscience in the development of public policies affecting young people is a blurring of three very different issues that need to be separated: (a) what science does and does not say about brain development in adolescence; (b) what neuroscience does and does not imply for the understanding of adolescent behavior; and (c) what these implications suggest for public policy. In this article, the author argues that a good deal is known about adolescent brain development, that this knowledge has in fact been useful in shaping our understanding of adolescent behavior, and that neuroscience, like behavioral science, can usefully inform policy discussions. He cautions, however, that nonexperts may be unduly swayed by neuroscience evidence and thus that such evidence should be presented with special care.

Sullivan, Christopher, et al. "Rebalancing Response to School-Based Offenses: A Civil Citation Program." *Youth Violence and Juvenile Justice* 8, no. 4 (2010): 279-294.

In recent years, zero-tolerance policies have been implemented in an attempt to reduce violent and/or drug-related activities in schools. These policies are sometimes expanded to include less serious crimes, which raises a number of questions regarding juvenile justice (JJ) system response and processing. This article discusses the need, implementation, and some preliminary program outcomes related to a civil citation (CC) process undertaken to provide an alternative to school-based justice referrals. Aggregate trends were reviewed based on internal program data as well as publicly available information. Follow-up data on CC youth were obtained and a matched sample of youth not engaged in the CC process was created using a state-level administrative data set to provide a preliminary assessment of outcomes. Key informant interviews examined program development and implementation. Results of this preliminary evaluation are considered in the larger context of youth diversion and school-based practices for dealing with youth misconduct.

Sullivan, Christopher, and Edward Latessa. "The Coproduction of Outcomes: An Integrated Assessment of Youth and Program Effects on Recidivism." *Youth Violence and Juvenile Justice* 9, no. 3 (2011): 191- 206.

In recent decades, states and communities have begun to utilize diversion programs as a means of preventing the unnecessary penetration of youth into the juvenile justice system and redirecting limited resources. Many of these diversion programs revolve around formal community-based programming. The authors utilize a large sample of youth (n = 4,325) nested in justice and treatment-related programs (n = 72) in order to jointly investigate the likelihood of recidivism based on youth risk and program characteristics. The analysis indicates that individual risk has a substantial effect on later recidivism, which is relatively constant across different programs. Programs do vary in their overall levels of recidivism. Measures of program type and integrity show few significant effects, however. Discussion of the results focuses on the general utility of such policies and the importance of considering the interaction between youth and programs in the production of key outcomes.

Swayze, Dana, and Danette Buskovick. "Youth in Minnesota Correctional Facilities: Responses to the 2010 Minnesota Student Survey." Minnesota

Dept. of Public Safety/Office of Justice Programs. St. Paul, MN: Statistical Analysis Center, 2011.

Results from a survey comparing youth in correctional facilities to youth in mainstream schools are presented. "Exploring differences between the two student groups can provide information on what challenges youth in correctional facilities are facing, and what targeted intervention efforts may alleviate their personal or situational difficulties. Similarly, areas in which survey responses are the same for both groups can illuminate protective factors all youth possess, or risk factors to which all youth are vulnerable" (p. 2). Sections of this report are: executive summary; introduction; findings regarding family connectedness, other social supports and community connectedness, school connectedness, school safety, alcohol, tobacco and other drug use, mental and emotional health, public safety, victimization, and sexual behavior; discussion and practice implications related to common protective factors, common risk factors, and risk factors unique to youth in correctional facilities; and conclusion. https://dps.mn.gov/divisions/ojp/formsdocuments/Documents/!2010%20 Youth%20Corrections%20Report.pdf

Toldson, Ivory A., et al. "Academic Potential Among African American Adolescents in Juvenile Detention Centers: Implications for Reentry to School." *Journal of Offender Rehabilitation* 49, no. 8 (Nov/Dec 2010): 551-570.

The study explores Black adolescent detainees' academic potential and motivation to return to school, to inform best practices and policies for juvenile reentry to educational settings. Adolescent detainees (N = 1,576) who were recruited from 1 male and 1 female youth detention facility, responded to surveys that assessed postdetention educational plans, as well as social and emotional characteristics, and criminal history. Multivariate analysis techniques were used to compare factors across race and gender, and plot linear relationships between key indicators of academic potential with associate factors. Findings revealed that youth were more likely to evince academic potential when they had a healthy level of self-esteem, adequate future goal orientation, positive mood, family and community involvement, fewer traumatic events, and less delinquent activity. [ABSTRACT FROM AUTHOR]

Vogel, Brenda, et al. "Arbitrary Arbitration: Diverting Juveniles into the Justice System-A Reexamination after 22 Years." *International Journal of*

Offender Therapy & Comparative Criminology 55, no. 4 (June 2011): 605-625.

[P]ublic policies with regard to sex offenders and the nature of their sexual offending assume that they are persistent specialists whose sexual offending is both recidivistic and dangerous. Yet, research on these assumptions is mixed, which leads some researchers to conclude that just about anything can be stated with regard to sex offenders. In an effort to overcome the limitations of previous research (highly select samples, short follow–up periods, lack of comparison group), the current study employs data from three birth cohorts from Racine, Wisconsin to examine the issue of juvenile to adult sex offending and its implications for current sex offender public policy. Policy Implications: Several results emerged from the current study. First, the fraction of juvenile sex offenders who committed adult sex offenses was quite small. Second, males who committed juvenile sex offenses were a tiny fraction of the cohort males who had a police contact for a juvenile offense. Third, the best predictor during a juvenile career for adult sex offending was the frequency of offending as a juvenile rather than whether a boy committed a sexual offense. Whether a male in Racine had a juvenile sex police contact contributed little to predicting his likelihood of adult sex offending. Specifically, 8.5% of males with juvenile sex police contacts had adult sex police contacts compared with 6.2% of males with any non–sex juvenile contact. With regard to policy, our findings also indicate that concentrating effort on those who were juvenile sex offenders will miss more than 90% of the cohort members who commit sex crimes as adults and will misidentify 90% of the targeted group of the juveniles as adult sex offenders. Such errors speak to the near impossibility of predicting which adolescent sex offenders will emerge as adult sex offenders and cast some doubt on the long–term predictive utility of juvenile sex offender registration. [ABSTRACT FROM AUTHOR]

Valentino, Amanda. *LGBTQ Youth in the Juvenile Justice System [Parts 1 and 2]* Chicago, IL: American Bar Association/Section of Litigation, 2011.

Issues surrounding justice-involved lesbian, gay, bisexual, transgender, and questioning/queer (LGBTQ) youth are discussed. It is vitally important for individuals working with youth to know that at least 13% of juveniles involved with the juvenile justice system are LGBTQ and require services and programs to address their particular needs and to keep them safe. Sections of Part 1 include: an increase in identifies LGBTQ

youth; disproportionate representation; examples of abuse; and that isolation may exacerbate the harm done to LGBTQ youth. Part 2 has sections addressing: discriminatory and inappropriate charges—the system's propensity to overcharge this population; constitutional rights; the right to equal protection; state nondiscrimination protections; and non-litigation strategies—education and awareness. http://apps.americanbar.org/litigation/committees/lgbt/articles/winter2011-valentino-juvenile-justice-system.html
http://apps.americanbar.org/litigation/committees/lgbt/articles/summer2011-multidimensionality-juvenile-justice.html

Ziedenberg, Jason, Imran Ahmad, and Shannon Wight. *Misguided Measures: The Outcomes and Impacts of Measure 11 on Oregon's Youth.* Washington, DC: Campaign for Youth Justice; Portland, OR: Partnership for Safety and Justice, 2011.
The effectiveness of Oregon's Measure 11 reveals the problems with trying juveniles as adults. "Measure 11 requires youth 15 years or older charged with one of 21 crimes to be prosecuted automatically in the adult criminal system and if convicted of that crime, to serve the same mandatory sentence that applies to adults" (p. 3). Nine chapters follow an executive summary: introduction—Measure 11 for juveniles, what we knew then, and what we know now; history— Measure 11 and automatic transfer in Oregon; overview—pathways to adult court for Oregon youth; outcomes—not guilty as charged; the disproportionate racial and ethnic impact of Measure 11; pretrial detention—adult jails or youth detention centers; aftermath—long-term impacts of adult convictions; public safety—Measure 11 did not make our communities safer; and recommendations. http://www.campaignforyouthjustice.org/documents/MisguidedMeasuresJuly2011.pdf

Ziedenberg, Jason. You're An Adult Now: Youth in Adult Criminal Justice Systems. 2011.
"It has been estimated that nearly 250,000 youth under age 18 end up in the adult criminal justice system every year. However, little attention has been directed to how adult corrections systems are managing the youth offenders that end up in jails, prisons and under community supervision. To address this information gap, the National Institute of Corrections (NIC) convened three dozen juvenile justice and adult corrections experts on June 18th, 2010, to consider some of the known issues, impacts and

opportunities that face corrections systems as they work to safely and effectively rehabilitate thousands of youth offenders in the nations' jails, prisons, probation and parole systems. This monograph presents the key findings identified during this convening of experts." Six section comprise this publication: executive summary; what is known about the issue of juveniles in the adult corrections systems, and where there are gaps in data collection and information; what the issues, impacts and options are facing public safety systems when youth are awaiting trial on adult charges; when youth are convicted, and committed to the adult system; when youth who convicted in adult court are on probation or parole; and conclusion--corrections and the entire public safety system needs to focus on the successful strategies to curb delinquency, and positive youth development. The "Summary of Options for Federal, State, and Local Policymakers to Consider" is appended. http://nicic.gov/Library/files/025555.pdf

JUVENILE JUSTICE: PROGRAMS FOR YOUNG WOMEN

Bell, Kelly, Mary A. Terzian, and Kristin A. Moore. What Works for Female Children and Adolescents: Lessons from Experimental Evaluations of Programs and Interventions. Washington, DC: Child Trends, 2012.

"Girls face unique developmental challenges in childhood and adolescence. Compared to boys, girls tend to report more mental health problems, and they are susceptible to reproductive health risks, such as unwanted pregnancy and sexually transmitted disease. While a number of evidence-based programs have been found to be effective at reducing risk factors for children and adolescents, many programs have differential impacts for girls and boys. Understanding what works for girls is critical to improving outcomes youth" (p. 1). This brief examines those programs that work or don't work for girls. Programs are rated according to found to work, mixed findings, and not found to work and are organized into the areas of academic achievement, delinquency, externalizing or acting out behaviors, mental health/internalizing (depression) outcomes, physical health and nutrition, reproduction health and sexuality, self-sufficiency, social skills, and substance use. http://www.childtrends.org/wp-content/uploads/2013/01/ChildTrends-2012 08 20 WW FemaleChildren Adol.pdf

Guiding Principles for Promising Female Programming: An Inventory of Best Practices. Washington, DC: U.S. Dept. of Justice, Office of Juvenile Justice and Delinquency Prevention, 2011.

This online guide "describes practical policy and program development processes and promising models... [addressing] female juvenile offenders, the problems they present, their needs, and our need to address them". Three chapters are contained in this publication: female juvenile delinquents—who they are and their needs; policy and program development for serving female juvenile delinquents; and comprehensive gender-specific services. An appendix provides a chart of promising programs.

http://www.ojjdp.gov/pubs/principles/contents.html

Roberts-Lewis, Amelia C., Chiquitia L. Welch-Brewer, Mary S. Jackson, Martin O. Pharr, and Sharon Parker. "Female Juvenile Offenders with Heart: Preliminary Findings of an Intervention Model for Female Juvenile Offenders with Substance Use Problems." *Journal of Drug Issues* 40, no. 3 (Summer 2010): 611-625.

This pilot study examined the effectiveness of an intensive, gender specific substance abuse treatment program, Holistic Enrichment for At-Risk Teens (HEART), on the psychosocial functioning of 30 incarcerated girls. A single-group multiple repeated measures design method was used to determine the effectiveness of the HEART program in reducing psychosocial problems associated with the behaviors of problem substance use and delinquency. The results showed that participants in the HEART program displayed significant improvement in eight of ten areas of psychosocial functioning: mental health, family relation, peer relations, educational status, vocational, leisure and recreational skills, and decreases in aggressive behaviors. The conclusion is that it is critical for juvenile correctional facilities to become sites where effective, empirically based treatment is provided. [PUBLICATION ABSTRACT]

Swayze, Dana, and Danette Buskovick. *Girls in Minnesota Correctional Facilities: Responses to the 2010 Minnesota Student Survey.* Minnesota Department of Public Safety. Office of Justice Programs. St. Paul, MN: Statistical Analysis Center, 2011.

"This report seeks to illuminate statistically significant differences in responses between girls and boys in correctional facilities; to explore how these data are relevant to research on juvenile justice risk factors by gender; and to provide research-based recommendations for serving the specific needs of juvenile female offenders" (p. 2). Sections following an executive summary are: introduction; findings for girls in Minnesota correctional facilities according to demographics, victimization, mental and emotional health, alcohol, tobacco and other drug use, family and community connectedness, school connectedness, delinquent behavior, and sexual behavior; discussion and practice implications for gender-responsive interventions—appropriate risk assessment, full continuum of services, and gender-responsive programming; and conclusion. https://dps.mn.gov/divisions/ojp/formsdocuments/Documents/!2010%20 Girls%20v%20Boys%20Corrections%20Report.pdf

Watson, Liz, and Peter Edelman. *Improving the Juvenile Justice System for Girls: Lessons from the States.* Washington, DC: Georgetown Center on Poverty, Inequality, and Public Policy, 2012.

Improving the Juvenile Justice System for Girls: Lessons from the States examines the challenges facing girls in the juvenile justice system and makes recommendations for gender-responsive reform at the local, state, and federal levels.

This report emerged from the policy series— marginalized Girls: Creating Pathways to Opportunity —convened by the Georgetown Center on Poverty, Inequality, and Public Policy, The National Crittenton Foundation, and the Human Rights Project for Girls. The series focuses on improving public systems' responses to the challenges facing marginalized girls and young women.

[From Executive Summary]

http://www.law.georgetown.edu/academics/centers-institutes /poverty-inequality/upload/JDS V1R4 Web Singles.pdf

Zavlek, Shelley, and Rebecca Maniglia. "Developing Correctional Facilities for Female Juvenile Offenders: Design and Programmatic Considerations." *Corrections Today* 69, no. 4 (Aug 2007): 58-63.

Research conducted by NCCD also identifies family fragmentation, academic failure, and health and mental health issues as some of the greatest concerns for girls and young at-risk women. The American Bar Association's report Justice by Gender affirmed the work of earlier research in identifying critical concerns that programmatic solutions must address: family problems, victimization both inside and outside the formal juvenile justice system, health and mental health issues, and school failure. OJJDP publications since the mid-1990s have made similar claims, citing substance abuse, teen pregnancy, academic failure, mental health needs, gang membership and societal pressure as issues of concern for this population, and academic studies have confirmed this standard list. In classrooms, multipurpose rooms and program spaces should be flexible to accommodate a variety of activities and teaching methods.

JUVENILE JUSTICE: FACILITIES

Against All Odds: Prison Conditions for Youth Offenders Serving Life without Parole Sentences in the United States. Human Rights Watch, 2012.

The conditions faced by juveniles sentenced to die in prisons are described. This report covers the breadth of a youth's life - from entering incarceration until they pass away. Five sections follow a summary and recommendations: introduction--potential for rehabilitation; physical harm and mistreatment in adult prisons; limited access to education and rehabilitation; psychological harm; and conclusion. "Youth offenders sentenced to life without parole enter prison while they are still growing up and deserve an opportunity to change. Brain science shows that youth are different from adults, their neurological systems still developing. Human rights law mandates that youth offenders be treated differently from adults and, to our knowledge, not a single youth offender is serving this sentence anywhere else in the world. Unfortunately, federal and state legislators in the United States continue to turn their backs on the science and remain out of step with practice elsewhere, forcing youth offenders serving life without parole to forfeit whatever their future might have held in store for them" (p. 1).

http://www.hrw.org/sites/default/files/reports/us0112ForUpload1.pdf

http://nicic.gov/Library/026519

Butts, Jeffrey A., Gladys Carrion, David Steinhart, and Jennifer Rodriguez. *Is the Juvenile Justice Realignment Train Slowing Down?* Kalamazoo, MI: National Center for Youth in Custody (NC4YC), 2012.

"After nearly two decades of falling crime, down-sizing juvenile corrections and detention is a central theme in a growing number of juvenile justice systems ... What does the future hold for juvenile justice reform? Were the changes that occurred over the past ten years a

permanent shift in policy and practice, or were they merely a temporary reaction to tight budgets and low rates of violent crime? Will policymakers maintain reforms if and when crime rises or budgets rebound?" Topics discussed include: the research consensus; states working to change juvenile justice from to; three basic strategies or levers for change; placement population are falling; why use so much commitment; key question for policy and practice; changing juvenile justice; policy issues; New York—keeping youth closer to home; performance measures for monitoring juvenile delinquent youth in New York; California juvenile justice realignment; staying focused on out destination—better outcomes for youth; and key principles for any change initiative. http://npjs.org/ncyc/documents/2013/09/is-the-juvenile-justice-realignment-train-slowingdown.pdf
http://nicic.gov/Library/026173

Daly, Reagan, Tarika Kapur, and Margaret Tarika. *Capital Change: A Process Evaluation of Washington, DC's Secure Juvenile Placement Reform.* New York: Vera Institute of Justice; Washington, DC: Center on Youth Justice, 2011.
Results from a year-long process evaluation of the District of Columbia's Department of Youth Rehabilitation Services (DYRS) are presented. The DYRS resulted from "a comprehensive reform of the District's responses to youth in secure placement (equivalent to prison in the adult context) (p. iii). Sections following an executive summary are: introduction; background—events leading to juvenile justice reform in DC; methodology; findings regarding DYRS's strategy for reform, components of the reform design, assessment of implementation, implementation as an ongoing process, and factors affecting cultural changes; recommendations for operations, staff development, and research and information-management; and conclusion. An appendix shows a timeline of reform benchmarks. The DYRS has made remarkable progress in implementing many elements of system reform. Yet, as with any comprehensive reform, there still remain some changes to be made.
http://www.vera.org/download?file=3191/Capital-Change-process-evaluation-DC-FINAL2.pdf http://nicic.gov/Library/024854

Deitch, Michele, Anna Lipton Galbraith, and Jordan Pollock. *Conditions for Certified Juveniles in Texas County Jails.* University of Texas at Austin. Lyndon B. Johnson School of Public Affairs, 2012.

This report aims to provide a clearer picture of the conditions for certified juveniles [juveniles transferred to the adult criminal justice system for trial] in county jails based on the findings of this survey. The report provides a comprehensive assessment of how certified juveniles are housed in county jails in Texas, and the challenges faced by jail administrators when they confine certified youth. This information should help inform juvenile boards ... and can also inform policy makers, state and county agencies, and advocates in future discussions about the most appropriate way to manage the confinement of certified juveniles" (p. ix). Five parts follow an executive summary: introduction; background; survey findings for number of certified juveniles in county jails, length of stay in county jails, housing, contact with adults, out-of-cell time, educational programming, and rehabilitative programming; discussion of survey findings; and recommendations. Many certified youth come in contact with adults when they are not being held in long-term isolation.
http://www.campaignforyouthjustice.org/documents/FRTX052012.pdf
http://nicic.gov/Library/026403

Growing Up Locked Down: Youth in Solitary Confinement in Jails and Prisons Across the United States. New York: American Civil Liberties Foundation; New York: Human Rights Watch, 2012.
"This report describes the needless suffering and misery that solitary confinement frequently inflicts on young people; examines the justifications that state and prison officials offer for using solitary confinement; and offers alternatives to solitary confinement in the housing and management of adolescents" (p. 2). Sections in addition to a summary and highlights of key recommendations are: background—kids in an adult system; how solitary confinement harms youth; youth in solitary confinement in adult facilities—corrections practices, numbers, and duration; violations of fundamental rights; and alternatives to the solitary confinement of youth; and recommendations.
http://www.hrw.org/sites/default/files/reports/us1012ForUpload.pdf
http://nicic.gov/Library/026674

How Can We Know If Juvenile Justice Reforms Are Worth the Cost? Washington, DC: Models for Change, 2011.
"This policy brief summarizes the benefit-cost analysis of a set of reforms intended to make juvenile detention more developmentally productive: residential centers that provide youths with group-based cognitive

behavior therapy" (p. 1). It offers great information for other agencies considering juvenile justice reform. Sections of this brief include: introduction; what should count as a benefit; what can be monetized; how costs should be quantified; and the Cook County Juvenile Temporary Detention Center (JTDC) study in which it is shown that cognitive behavior therapy (CBT) has modest impact at very low costs. http://www.modelsforchange.net/publications/320
http://nicic.gov/Library/026078

Kinker, Jeannette. "Successful Management of Juvenile Residential Facilities: A Performance Based Approach." *Corrections Today* 72, no. 5 (Oct 2010): 101.

In its introduction, Successful Management of Juvenile Residential Facilities: A Performance Based Approach, includes a descriptive list of problems identified in one state's troubled juvenile facility. I'm sure that if this list were to be shown to other juvenile justice professionals across the country, some would be surprised, while others would identify with their struggles.

Macomber, Donna, et al. "Education in Juvenile Detention Facilities in the State of Connecticut: A Glance at the System." *Journal of Correctional Education* 61, no. 3 (Sep 2010): 223-261.

The state of Connecticut detained 1,444 children and youth and committed approximately 270 to the Department of Children and Families for out of home placement in the 2007-2008 calendar year. A significant number of children and youth have special education needs that are often unidentified by home school districts. State and federal law mandate the provision of special education and related services to this population. In addition, education of these individuals is imperative as research indicates educational success is a key component for decreasing recidivism (relapse into unlawful activity) rates and providing opportunities toward productive adulthood. The cost of recidivism to detention is not only monetary; criminal misconduct also threatens the safety of society members as well. The Yale University Child Study Center under the auspices of the Connecticut Judicial Branch, Court Support Services Division (CSSD) conducted a situational analysis of the juvenile detention centers and community residential centers. The focus of this analysis was to: (1) describe the educational characteristics of detained children and youth; (2) describe the educational programs currently used in detention and assess whether the educational programming provided is consistent with the framework of the State of Connecticut Department of Education; (3) typify the community of teachers working with students in detention, identify systemic obstacles and/or challenges to educating this population, ascertain the pathways of educational records of detained children and youth; and (4) identify system barriers or challenges to delivering education to this population and teaching in detention or alternative to detention settings. This report is a summary of findings. [PUBLICATION ABSTRACT]

Marksamer, Jody, Dean Spade, and Gabriel Arkles. *A Place of Respect: A Guide for Group Care Facilities Serving Transgender and Gender Non-Conforming Youth.* San Francisco, CA: National Center for Lesbian Rights; New York: Sylvia Rivera Law Project, 2011.
"Transgender and gender non-conforming youth often face serious physical, emotional, and sexual abuse in group homes, detention centers, and correctional institutions. Because staff members are often unsure of how to provide respectful and supportive services to these youth, they may unwittingly subject them to situations that are discriminatory and harmful. This guide offers group care facilities information and tools to provide transgender and gender nonconforming young people with appropriate and informed care" (p. 2). Five chapters are contained in this publication: understanding transgender and gender non-conforming youth; the challenges of living with a stigmatized identity; group care facilities' legal responsibility to treat transgender and gender non-conforming youth fairly and keep them safe; best practices for working with transgender and gender non-conforming youth; and best practices for administrators for changing culture, adopting practice guidelines and policies, and training and evaluating staff. An appendix provides the "Model Policy & Practice Guidelines for Providing Non-Discriminatory Services to LGBT [Lesbian, Gay, Bisexual, Transgender] and Gender Non-Conforming Youth in Group Care Facilities".

McDaniel, Sara, Kristen M. Heil, David E. Houchins, and Ellen L. Duchaine. "A Guide to Implementing Response to Intervention in Long-term Residential Juvenile Justice Schools." *Journal of Correctional Education* 62, no. 1 (Mar 2011): 51-68.
Since the passage of the Individuals with Disabilities Education Improvement Act (2004), public schools have been permitted to use a response to intervention model to address academic and social problems

of students and identify students with disabilities. As the collective educational community tackles implementation of response to intervention in mainstream public schools, minimal attention has been provided to juvenile justice school settings. The purpose of this paper is to provide juvenile justice professionals with guidance on how to implement response to intervention in their school setting. Emphasis is placed on the long-term facilities and the use of a multi-disciplinary approach. Suggested guidelines and unique considerations are discussed and a student scenario is provided to illustrate response to intervention implementation. [PUBLICATION ABSTRACT]

Mendel, Richard A. *No Place for Kids: The Case for Reducing Juvenile Incarceration*. Baltimore, MD: Annie E. Casey Foundation, 2011.
The critical need for juvenile corrections reform is explained. This report should be read by anyone interested in issues surrounding juveniles involved in the criminal justice system. Sections of this publication clarifies: what is wrong with juvenile corrections facilities in the U.S.—dangerous, ineffective, unnecessary, obsolete, wasteful, and inadequate; whether it is safe to reduce the number of juveniles confined; how states should go about reforming juvenile corrections—six priorities; and embracing better policies, programs, and practices in juvenile corrections. "The time has come for states to embrace a fundamentally different orientation to treating adolescent offenders—an approach grounded in evidence that promises to be far more humane, cost-effective, and protective of public safety than our time-worn and counterproductive reliance on juvenile incarceration" (p. 4).
http://www.aecf.org/OurWork/JuvenileJustice/JuvenileJusticeReport.aspx

National Council on Crime and Delinquency. *Juvenile Detention in Cook County: Future Directions*. Oakland, CA: NCCD, 2011.
Results from an assessment of Cook County's youth detention practices are presented. "This study looks beyond the challenges of the current facility to examine more fundamentally the detention needs of the county and its youth. The ultimate goal of the study is to guide discussion regarding a new vision for detention in Cook County—a vision that holds to the ideals that informed the creation of the court in 1899 while recognizing the current circumstances in which the court operates" (p. 4). Sections following an executive summary include: introduction and background; detention population and practice; program maintenance;

physical facility; information systems; and summary recommendations. Appendixes provide information about: the Cook County Screening Form; disproportionate minority contact (DMC) reduction cycle; outline of educational assessment needs; and data-mining experiences. http://www.nccdglobal.org/sites/default/files/publicationpdf/cook-county-report.pdf

Oesterreich, Heather A, Sara McNie Flores. "Learning to C: Visual Arts Education as Strengths Based Practice in Juvenile Correctional Facilities." *Journal of Correctional Education* 60, no. 2 (Jun 2009): 146- 162.
Strength-based approaches, originating in juvenile justice as early as the late 1800s, situate the work of juvenile correctional facilities as assisting youth in utilizing their strengths and competencies to understand how they can be applied their lives to affect change and growth.
While strengths-based approaches might have originated philosophically in juvenile justice they have not persisted in practice. In this qualitative case study of an art program in a juvenile correctional facility, visual arts acts a bridge between philosophy and practice to demonstrate how strength-based practices can affect change and growth with incarcerated youth. Specifically, this study demonstrates how visual arts education as a strength-based practice in juvenile correctional facilities offers youth the opportunity for change and growth to occur when their strengths, past successes, present behaviors and possible futures emerge. Specifically, visual arts education is situated as strength-based practice that allows young men who are incarcerated to "scc" themselves actively engage in the 5 C's-connection, community, contribution, concentration, and completion. [PUBLICATION ABSTRACT]

A Quick Guide for LGBTI Policy Development for Youth Confinement Facilities. Washington, DC: The Moss Group, Inc, 2012.
"This Quick Guide will help agencies and facilities develop a comprehensive response to working with lesbian, gay, bisexual, transgender and intersex (LGBTI) youth. It is not meant to provide an answer to every question or an in-depth discussion of all issues that agencies face or that the LGBTI population faces while in custody. It provides an overview of the important issues that agencies should consider when working to house and treat LGBTI youth in a way that is safe and consistent with an agency's mission, values, and security guidelines ... This Quick Guide is organized chronologically according to the decisions

an agency will have to make before and at the point when an LGBTI youth enters the system. These areas of focus include: Assessment of Agency Culture (as relates to LGBTI individuals); Assessment of Agency Staff and Administration Knowledge and Attitudes; Examination of Current Relevant Agency Norms; Development and Implementation Mechanisms; Development of Awareness of Current Legal Responsibilities; Foundational Issues; Intake Screening/Risk Assessment; Classification and Housing Placement; Medical and Mental Health Care; Information Management; Group Youth Management; Specific Safety and Privacy Concerns for Transgender and Intersex Youth; and Staff, Volunteer, and Contractor Training Requirements" (p. 1).
http://nicic.gov/Library/files/026701.pdf

Risler, Ed, and Tom O'Rourke. "Thinking Exit at Entry: Exploring Outcomes of Georgia's Juvenile Justice Educational Programs." *Journal of Correctional Education* 60, no. 3 (Sep 2009). 225-239.
Educational programs are often considered the last opportunity for an incarcerated youth to prepare for successful transition into society. While there is considerable literature identifying and describing the characteristics of youth and program services for youth in correctional facilities, it is important to gain a better understanding of factors that lead to successful transitioning upon return to their home communities. This purpose of this article is to provide an overview of the educational programs in correctional facilities operated by the Georgia Department of Juvenile Justice, and to report on the findings of a follow-up study exploring the outcomes of a cohort of youth that completed an educational program and received either a High School Diploma, a Special Education Diploma, or a GED. [PUBLICATION ABSTRACT]

JUVENILE JUSTICE: TRAINING

An Executive Summary: Rethinking Juvenile Justice. Washington, DC: Models for Change, 2011.
This brief provides a very nice summary of the book "Rethinking Juvenile Justice" by Elizabeth S. Scott and Laurence Steinberg. "They outline a new development model that is complex, nuanced, and grounded in scientific evidence" (p. 1). This publication explains why it is a great time for reform—we know more about adolescent development, public

attitudes are changing, and incarcerating juveniles is not very cost-effective. This summary also discusses: fairness and the principle of proportionality, drawing age boundaries, and what to do with juveniles who are repeat offenders.
http://www.modelsforchange.net/publications/321
http://nicic.gov/Library/025647

Arthur, Pat, and Christopher Hartney. *Arkansas Youth Justice: The Architecture of Reform.* National Council on Crime and Delinquency (NCCD). Oakland, CA: National Center for Youth Law, 2012.
"Arkansas leaders, like their counterparts in other states, have embarked on a planned course to transform the state's juvenile justice system. They aim to ensure that youth are not inappropriately or unnecessarily held in costly secure confinement, and that taxpayer dollars are spent wisely on services that actually produce good outcomes for youth, families, and the community" (p. 1). This report documents their efforts in this endeavor. It is a useful tool if your state is looking to reform your own juvenile justice system. Sections comprising this document include: introduction; the past; on the road to reform; building the vision; successes so far; the road ahead; hypothetical future reform scenarios; and conclusion and recommendations. Arkansas has reduced commitments to state custody by 20%, average length of stay by 19%, and secure juvenile facility beds by 30%.
http://www.nccdglobal.org/sites/default/files/publicationpdf/arkansas-youth-justice.pdf http://nicic.gov/Library/026044

Bringing Youth Home: A National Movement to Increase Public Safety, Rehabilitate Youth and Save Money. Washington, DC: National Juvenile Justice Network, 2011.
"This paper includes examples of states that have reduced their juvenile facility populations and are now not only reaping the rewards of new found funds that can be redirected into more effective community-based services for youth, but also seeing a better return on their investment in terms of juvenile rehabilitation and public safety" (p. 1). States highlighted are Alabama, California, the District of Columbia, Florida, Kansas, New York, Ohio, and Texas. Things to consider when downsizing juvenile populations include: treat youth appropriately; reevaluate which youth are being incarcerated; stay focused on disproportionate minority

contact; ensure accountability; keep youth in homelike settings; and redirect funds to alternatives to confinement.
http://nicic.gov/Library/025317

Families Unlocking Futures: Solutions to the Crisis in Juvenile Justice. Oakland, CA: Justice for Families (J4F) DataCenter, 2012.
The work of this report and the work of Justice for Families is designed to set the record straight: to correct misperceptions about system-involved youth and their families; to demonstrate the depth of engagement by system-involved youth and their families; and to assert the critical need for these families' active participation and leadership in re-designing the youth justice system in order to secure safer and more prosperous communities" (p. 10-11). The following sections are contained in this report: justice systems lock down youth and lock out families—locked down/locked out of schools, booking (arrest), detention, the courtroom, probation, youth prisons, and youth re-entry; juvenile justice systems tear apart families and destabilize communities through economics, mental and emotional health, and feelings of isolation, alienation, and powerlessness; families demand solutions since families are the solution; Justice for Families Blueprint for Youth Justice Transformation; and conclusion—a call to action.
http://njjn.org/uploads/digital-library/FamiliesUnlockingFuturesFULLNOEMBARGO.pdf?utmsource=NJJN%27s+10th+Annual+Forum+Advances + Juvenile+Justice+Reform&utm campaign=Newsletter%3A+Sept13%2C+2012 &utmmedium=email
http://nicic.gov/Library/026529

Glick, Barry, and John C. Gibbs. Aggression Replacement Training: A Comprehensive Intervention for Aggressive Youth. Champaign, IL: Research Press, 2011.
This book "clarifies the theory behind the ART interventions, gives user-friendly suggestions for successful implementation, and offers step-by-step session plans for conducting the 10-week training program." ART – Aggression Replacement Training – teaches the youth how to positively deal with their frustration and anger. This manual is divided into two parts. Part I, ART program content and implementation, covers: ART components and implementation concerns; social skills training—the behavioral component of ART; anger control training—the affective component of ART; moral reasoning—the cognitive component of ART;

group member motivation and resistance; enhancing generalization of performance; application models and evaluation of program effectiveness; and program administration and management. Part II, ART sessions, explains how to deliver each of the components during the 10-week program. The included CD provides copies of each reproducible form and handout contained in this book.

Lesbian, Gay, Bisexual, Transgender, Questioning and Intersex (LGBTQI) Youth. Washington: District of Columbia Department of Youth Rehabilitation Services, 2012.
"The purpose of this policy is to provide a safe, healthy, accepting environment for lesbian, gay, bisexual, transgender, questioning and intersex (LGBTQI) youth, and to prevent harassment and discrimination against youth who self-identity or are perceived as LGBTQI" (p. 1). Procedures cover: positive youth development; confidentiality; intake and classification; names and language; clothing and gender presentation; bathrooms and showers; medical and mental health care; searches; training of employees; youth education; and responding to harassment and discrimination.

Page, Joshua, and Shelly Schaefer. "From Risks to Assets: Toward a Strengths-Based Approach to Juvenile Reentry into the Community." *CURA Reporter* 41 no. 1 (2011): 34-41.
Strategies for making juvenile reentry more effective are described. Such information is vital if a juvenile agency is trying to reform itself into a successful organization. Sections of this article include: probation officer and probationer—a pivotal relationship for the juvenile offender's transition into the community; risk/needs-based versus strengths-based approach; research methodology; case studies; and discussion. A strengths-based approach focuses on juveniles' strengths or assets, provides encouragement and support, fosters empowerment, and collaborates with them on ways to reach their goals.
http://www.jjcmn.com/public/2011/05/Toward-a-Strengths-Based-Approach-to-JuvenileJustice-Reentry.pdf
http://nicic.gov/Library/025238

Wilber, Shannan, Bernadette Brown, and Anthony Celestine. *LGBT Youth in Detention: Understanding and Integrating Equitable Services.*

Washington, DC: Juvenile Detention Alternative Initiative. The Equity Project, 2012.
This presentation is comprised of a series of questions regarding: what is known about LGBT youth; intake and risk assessment; gender and sexual orientation; name and pronoun; detention and family involvement; housing; and race. The resulting discussion results in covering: the available data on lesbian, gay, bisexual and gender nonconforming (LGBT) youth in detention; implications for practice; and integration of these issues in site-based reform efforts. http://www.jdaihelpdesk.org/intersiteconf2012/LGBT%20Youth%20In%20Detention%20Understanding%20and%20Integrating%20Equitable%20Services%20(2012%20Conference).pdf

National Conference of State Legislatures. *Juvenile Justice Guide Book for Legislators.* Denver, CO: National Conference of State Legislatures, 2011.
Individuals needing a review of the most pressing issues impacting juvenile justice should refer to this guidebook. "This juvenile justice primer highlights significant research, program approaches and gives examples of state legislation." Sections contained in this publication are: introduction and overview; adolescent development and competency; delinquency prevention and intervention; indigent defense, counsel, and procedural issues; mental health needs of juvenile offenders; disproportionate minority contact; Medicaid for juvenile justice-involved children; reentry and aftercare; cost-benefit analysis of juvenile justice programs; and references, glossary, and resources.
http://www.ncsl.org/default.aspx?tabid=23850

JUVENILE JUSTICE: WEBSITES

Advancing Evidence Based Practice, http://www.advancingebp.org/
A nonprofit association of program providers, program developers, researchers, intermediary agencies, government agencies, and policy makers all working to promote evidence-based programs for at-risk youth. Our mission is to broaden the availability of research-proven programs to better the lives of kids.

Center on Juvenile and Criminal Justice, http://www.cjcj.org/index.html

The Center on Juvenile and Criminal Justice (CJCJ) is a non-profit nonpartisan organization whose mission is to reduce society's reliance on incarceration as a solution to social problems. In pursuit of this mission, CJCJ provides direct services, technical assistance, and policy analysis that work in unison to promote a balanced and humane criminal justice system designed to reduce incarceration and enhance long-term public safety.

Center for Juvenile Justice Reform (Georgetown University), http://cjjr.georgetown.edu/

The Center for Juvenile Justice Reform at Georgetown University's Public Policy Institute is designed to support leaders in the juvenile justice and related systems of care. The Center seeks to complement the good work being done across the country in juvenile justice reform by providing a multi-systems perspective and set of resources in support of this work.

Coalition for Juvenile Justice, http://www.juvjustice.org/

The Coalition for Juvenile Justice (CJJ) is a nationwide coalition of State Advisory Groups (SAGs) and allies dedicated to preventing children and youth from becoming involved in the courts and upholding the highest standards of care when youth are charged with wrongdoing and enter the justice system. CJJ envisions a nation where fewer children are at risk of delinquency; and if they are at risk or involved with the justice system, they and their families receive every possible opportunity to live safe, healthy and fulfilling lives.

Council of Juvenile Correctional Administrators, http://cjca.net/

The Council of Juvenile Correctional Administrators (CJCA) is a national non-profit organization, formed in 1994 to improve local juvenile correctional services, programs and practices so the youths within the systems succeed when they return to the community and to provide national leadership and leadership development for the individuals responsible for the systems. CJCA represents the youth correctional CEOs in 50 states, Puerto Rico and major metropolitan counties.

Crime Solutions, http://www.crimesolutions.gov/

The Office of Justice Programs' CrimeSolutions.gov uses rigorous research to determine what works in criminal justice, juvenile justice, and crime victim services. In addition to continuing to capture ongoing reviews of justice programs, CrimeSolutions.gov now also presents reviews of justice practices. A practice is a general category of activities, strategies, or procedures that share similar characteristics with regard to the issues they address and how they address them. While CrimeSolutions.gov program profiles can answer questions like "Did the ABC Mentoring Program in Anytown, USA achieve its goals?", a practice profile might be used to answer "Does mentoring usually achieve its goals?"

Journal of Juvenile Justice, http://www.journalofjuvjustice.org/
The Journal of Juvenile Justice is a semi-annual, peer-reviewed journal sponsored by the Office of Juvenile Justice and Delinquency Prevention (OJJDP). Articles address the full range of issues in juvenile justice, such as juvenile victimization, delinquency prevention, intervention, and treatment.

Juvenile Justice Bill Tracking Database, http://www.ncsl.org/default.aspx?tabid=12686
NCSL has partnered with the John D. and Catherine T. MacArthur Foundation to develop this juvenile justice legislation database. Search 2008 through 2013 legislation by State; Topic; Key Word; Year; Status; or Primary Sponsor.

Juvenile Detention Alternatives Initiative, http://www.jdaihelpdesk.org/default.aspx
JDAI is based upon eight core, interconnected strategies that address the primary reasons why youth are unnecessarily or inappropriately detained. It is necessary that all core strategies be intentionally and effectively applied in order to achieve maximum results in reduction of detention populations. Scroll through each of the eight core strategies by clicking on the arrows, and then select by clicking on the strategy name. If you are unable to locate specific information please submit your question to the Help Desk.

Juvenile Justice Information Exchange. Center for Sustainable Journalism. Juvenile Justice Information Exchange, 2012. http://jjie.org
"Focused not just on delivering information, but rather on an 'exchange' of ideas, the Juvenile Justice Information Exchange fosters a community

of support around the issues facing the youth of our country. Members are made up of people like yourself who are interested in doing what is best for at-risk kids, along with industry professionals who work with children on a daily basis and citizens of Georgia and around the United States. Doing what is best for children means staying well informed on governmental policies and legislation, court rulings, educational trends, treatment, research, prevention programs and other factors that impact the quality of service delivered to the kids that need them most."

Juvenile Justice Trainers Association, http://www.jjta.org/

The Juvenile Justice Trainers Association is an organization devoted to the development and advancement of a specialized system of education and training for juvenile justice professionals. Composed primarily of staff development and training specialists, the association provides a national network for sharing information, providing technical services and developing other support mechanisms for juvenile justice trainers.

Model Programs Guide: http://www.ojjdp.gov/mpg/

The MPG is designed to assist practitioners and communities in implementing evidence-based prevention and intervention programs that can make a difference in the lives of children and communities. The MPG database of over 200 evidence-based programs covers the entire continuum of youth services from prevention through sanctions to reentry. The MPG can be used to assist juvenile justice practitioners, administrators, and researchers to enhance accountability, ensure public safety, and reduce recidivism. The MPG is an easy-to-use tool that offers a database of scientifically-proven programs that address a range of issues, including substance abuse, mental health, and education programs.

National Center for Juvenile Justice, http://www.ncjj.org/

The National Center for Juvenile Justice (NCJJ), located in Pittsburgh, PA. is the research division of the National Council of Juvenile and Family Court Judges and is the oldest juvenile justice research group in the United States, having conducted national and sub national studies on crime and delinquency since 1973.

National Center for State Courts: Juvenile Justice and Delinquency Resource Guide http://www.ncsc.org/Topics/Children-Families-and-Elders/Juvenile-Justice-andDelinquency/Resource-Guide.aspx

National Council on Crime & Delinquency, http://www.nccdglobal.org/what-we-do

At NCCD, we envision a just society in which people are safe and supported in their communities and treated with dignity by the systems that serve them. Our mission is to promote just and equitable social systems for individuals, families, and communities through research, public policy, and practice. For over 100 years, our research has informed better system responses at all points of contact. We work to help protect children from abuse and neglect, to create safe and rehabilitative justice systems for youth and adults, and to address the needs of older adults and adults with disabilities. Within these systems we also study the unique concerns of girls, LGBT individuals, and overrepresented racial and ethnic groups.

National Juvenile Justice and Delinquency Prevention Coalition (NJJDPC), http://juvjustice.njjn.org/initiative njjdpc.html

The Coalition for Juvenile Justice (CJJ) envisions a nation where fewer children are at risk of delinquency; and if they are at risk or involved with the justice system, they and their families receive every possible opportunity to live safe, healthy and fulfilling lives.

National Juvenile Justice Evaluation Center, http://www.jrsa.org/njjec/

The National Juvenile Justice Evaluation Center (NJJEC) assists state, local, and tribal entities with the evaluation of juvenile justice programs and implementation of evidence-based initiatives. We provide a number of resources to guide juvenile justice agencies and practitioners to select, implement, evaluate, and sustain programs supported by research evidence.

National Juvenile Justice Network, http://www.njjn.org/

The National Juvenile Justice Network (NJJN) exists to support and enhance the work of state-based groups to promote the reform of America's critically flawed juvenile justice system at every level. Through education, community-building and leadership development, NJJN enhances the capacity of juvenile justice coalitions and organizations in 33 states to press for state and federal laws, policies and practices that are fair, equitable and developmentally appropriate for all children, youth and families involved in, or at risk of becoming involved in, the justice system.

National Partnership for Juvenile Services, http://npjs.org/
The Partnership joins the Council for Juvenile Detention, Council for Juvenile Corrections, Council for Educators of At-Risk and Delinquent Youth, and Council for Juvenile Justice Trainers - NPJS supports and advocates for juvenile services practitioners, including direct care staff, teachers, staff trainers, and administrators, in secure and non-secure programs? - See more at: http://npjs.org/#sthash.9X8geBsJ.dpuf

Office of Juvenile Justice and Delinquency Prevention/National Training and Technology Assistance Center, https://www.nttac.org/index.cfm

PREA in the Juvenile Justice System. National PREA Resource Workgroup. Salem: Oregon Youth Authority, 2011.
Resources related to the Prison Rape Elimination Act (PREA) and its application to juvenile corrections can be found at this website. If you are looking for PREA in juvenile settings this is the first place you should look. There are pointers to publications, useful links, training materials and samples (laws, policies, rules and procedures, trainings, and tools/materials; and other resources.
http://www.oregon.gov/OYA/prea/prearesources.shtml

Juvenile Sex Offenders

Aebi, Marcel, Gunnar Vogt, Belinda Plattner, Hans-Christoph Steinhausen, and Cornelia Bessler. "Offender Types and Criminality Dimensions in Male Juveniles Convicted of Sexual Offenses." *Sexual Abuse: A Journal of Research & Treatment* 24, no. 3 (Sep 2012): 265-288.
Previous studies have described juveniles who sexually offended (JSO) as a rather heterogeneous population. In consequence, different typologies of JSO have been proposed for a better understanding of the causes and interventional needs of JSO. Three previously described types have received support in previous studies, namely, the victim age type (JSO offending against children vs. adolescents or adults), the co-offender status type (JSO offending as singles vs. in groups), and the crime history type (JSO with vs. without a previous history of crime). The validity of

these types is tested in a consecutive sample of 223 criminal male adolescents, who had been convicted of a sexual offense between 2000 and 2008 in the Canton of Zurich (Switzerland). By analyzing nine offender characteristics, four victim characteristics and six offense characteristics, the best evidence is found for the victim age–based type. The co-offender status and the crime history types are less well supported. However, all three types are related to each other and do not provide a comprehensive characterization of JSO. Therefore, an additional principal component analyses is performed searching for basic dimensions of juvenile sexual delinquency and leading to the following factors: "single offender with severe molestation of a related child," "persistent general delinquent with migrant background," "older offender with alcohol use and familial constraints," "multiple and aggressive offender with social adversities," and "offender with unselected and multiple victims." These five dimensions reflect different relevant factors of sexual offending behavior in male juveniles and may have further impact on forensic and clinical practice. [ABSTRACT FROM AUTHOR]

Burkhart, Barry, Allen Peaton, and Ray Sumrall. "Youth Services Teams With Universities For Sex Offender Programs." *Corrections Today* 71, no. 3 (Jun 2009): 93-94.

The first of these was a requirement that the agency, DYS, hold the partnership to a standard of excellence. [...] DYS was determined to provide sufficient resources that the program would have a real opportunity to meet a criterion of excellence. [...] at posttreatment, the juvenile sex offenders showed an increase in delinquency measures due to their exposure to the general delinquent population.

Caldwell, Michael F. Casey Dickinson. "Sex Offender Registration and Recidivism Risk in Juvenile Sexual Offenders." *Behavioral Sciences & the Law* 27, no. 6 (Nov/Dec 2009): 941-956.

Juvenile sex offenders are increasingly included in sex offender registration laws, based, in part, on the assumption that they pose a distinctively high risk for future sexual violence and registration may help to mitigate this risk. To test this assumption, the current study compares risk scores on the static scales of the Juvenile Sex Offender Assessment Protocol—II (JSOAP-II; Prentky & Righthand, <BIBR>2003</BIBR>) and the Youth Level of Service/Case Management Inventory (YLS/CMI; Hoge, Andrews, & Leschied, 2002), between samples of 106 registered and 66 unregistered juvenile sex offenders. New criminal charges, including sexually based crimes, were examined over a mean follow-up of 49.2 months (SD = 29.6 months). Results indicated that registered youth had lower risk scores on scales that most accurately predicted recidivism and registered youth were charged with new crimes at rates similar to those of unregistered youth. Reoffense risk, as measured by the risk scales, was not moderated by registration. The findings did not support the assumption that registration can effectively lower the risk for reoffense in juvenile offenders. [ABSTRACT FROM AUTHOR]

Calley, Nancy G. "Juvenile Sex Offenders and Sex Offender Legislation: Unintended Consequences." *Federal Probation* 72, no. 39 (Dec 2008): 37-41.

The article focuses on the unintended consequences of the legislation on juvenile sex offender. The legislation established a national registry for sex offenders including juvenile offenders of 14 years of age or older. The registry of juvenile sex offender, according to the author, has sparked a controversy and legal attempts have been made to avoid registration. He concludes that actions to avoid registration may inadvertently prohibit treatment opportunities.

Fanniff, Amanda M. and Elizabeth J. Letourneau. "Sexual Abuse: Another Piece of the Puzzle: Psychometric Properties of the J-SOAP-II." *Journal of Research & Treatment* 24, no. 4 (Dec 2012): 378- 408.

The authors reviewed nine studies examining psychometric properties of the Juvenile Sex Offender Assessment Protocol–II (J-SOAP-II) and examined the psychometric properties of the JSOAP-II when items were scored based on probation records obtained at or near disposition and prior to treatment. Data from 73 boys ages 12 to 17 who participated in a larger randomized clinical trial informed this study. Reliability (internal consistency and interrater agreement) and validity (concurrent, discriminant, and predictive) were examined. Scale 1, Sexual Drive/Preoccupation, was characterized by adequate reliability and concurrent validity but did not predict scores on a measure of concerning sexual behavior. This is consistent with seven studies that failed to find evidence of predictive validity using measures of sexual recidivism. Also consistent with the literature, Scale 2, Impulsive/Antisocial Behavior, performed well with respect to nearly all psychometric properties including predictive validity. Review of remaining scales and scores and clinical policy implications are discussed. [ABSTRACT FROM PUBLISHER]

Fanniff, Amanda M., and David J. Kolko. "Victim Age-Based Subtypes of Juveniles Adjudicated for Sexual Offenses: Comparisons Across Domains in an Outpatient Sample." *Sexual Abuse: A Journal of Research & Treatment* 24, no. 3 (Sep 2012): 224-264.

Adolescents adjudicated for sexual offenses are a heterogeneous group. The identification of more homogeneous subgroups of offenders may enable improved treatment, as the specific risks and needs presented by each group could be more effectively targeted. The current study examines three subgroups derived based on the age of victim(s), a popular method of subtyping that has mixed empirical support, using a sample of 176 males adjudicated for a sexual offense and court-ordered to participate in a community-based collaborative intervention program that integrates treatment and probationary services. Differences expected between groups based on theories regarding victim-age based subtypes are examined, in addition to differences consistently identified in prior research. Results indicate that these three subgroups are more similar than different, although some expected differences were found. Juveniles with child victims were more likely to have male victims and biologically related victims. Juveniles with peer/adult victims were more likely to have poor monitoring by their parents and more likely to have been arrested again. Juveniles with mixed types of victims appeared similar to juveniles with child victims on some variables and similar to those with peer/adult victims on others. Treatment implications and future directions for research are discussed. Typologies based on clinical characteristics of the youth rather than offense characteristics may have more promise for identifying meaningful subgroups.

Galley, Nancy G. "New Directions in Juvenile Sex Offender Management: Designing a Collaborative Approach." *Federal Probation* 73, no. 3 (Dec 2009): 50-56, 72.

[...] over the past decade, while these percentages have remained largely consistent (Barbaree &Marshall, 2006), there has been considerable growth in the literature in specific aspects of juvenile sex offending, such as assessment (Calley, 2007; Grisso &Underwood, 2004; O'Reilly &Carr, 2006; Prentky, Harris, Frizzell, &Righthand, 2000; Worling &Curwen, 2001) and treatment (Prentky, Harris, Frizzell, &Righthand, 2000; Witt,

Boslye, Hiscox, 2002; Worling &Curwen, 2001), and to a lesser degree, research has been dedicated to issues such as modus operandi (Bijleveld, Weerman, Looije, &Hendriks, 2007; Burton, 2003; Veneziano, Veneziano, &LeGrand, 2003), issues related to legislative changes (Petrosino &Petrosino, 1999; Vasquez, Maddan, &Walker, 2008), and specific legal challenges (Hiller, 1998; Trivits &Reppucci, 2002; Turoff, 2001). [...] whereas sex offenders comprise just one sub-group of the criminal population, other offenders with specialized needs (e.g., co-occurring mental health disorders, developmentally disabled individuals, young adults/older teens) may benefit equally from such comprehensive and collaborative approaches to system improvement that are specifically designed to address their unique needs.

Gillis, H. L.; Gass, Michael A. "Treating Juveniles in a Sex Offender Program Using Adventure-Based Programming: A Matched Group Design." *Journal of Child Sexual Abuse* 19 no. 1 (Jan/Feb 2010): 20-34.
Ninety-five male juvenile sex offenders in an adventure-based behavior management program (LEGACY) were matched with male juveniles in state treatment-as-usual and other specialized programs in the same state to determine program effectiveness (as measured by rearrest rates). The LEGACY program demonstrated significant treatment effectiveness on rearrest rates when compared with youth development centers and other specialized programs two and three years later. Overall, three-year rearrest rates for the most serious reoffenses for each of the placements were as follows: 34.8% for YDC, 32.6% for OSP, and 19% for LEGACY

Gunby, Clare, and Jessica Woodhams. "Sexually Deviant Juveniles: Comparisons Between the Offender and Offence Characteristics of 'Child Abusers' and 'Peer Abusers'." *Psychology, Crime & Law* 16, no. 1,2 (2010): 47-64.
The last decade has seen increased concern regarding the sexual offences committed by young people. In line with this concern is an interest in developing an empirical research base that can help identify typologies of juvenile sex offenders and, in turn, direct resources. The current study investigated whether youths who sexually offend against children (individuals at least 5 years younger than themselves) differ in terms of offender and offence variables from juveniles who sexually assault members of their peer group. Findings were developed from data extracted from 43 files held by local Youth Offending Teams. Perpetrators of abuse

were all male and were aged from 10 to 17 years. Findings indicated that juvenile child abusers experienced greater deficits in self-esteem and social isolation. In contrast, peer abusers had witnessed family violence more frequently and had family members associated with criminal activity more often. Logistic regression analysis found the variables of 'knowing the victim', 'lacking age appropriate friends', and 'having been the victim of bullying' all reliably predicted offender status (child vs. peer). Findings suggest different typologies of juvenile sex offenders may have different routes to abusive behaviour and therefore require interventions that are tailored to their criminogenic needs.

Hendriks, Jan and Catrien Bijleveld. “Recidivism Among Juvenile Sex Offenders After Residential Treatment.” *Journal of Sexual Aggression* 14, no. 1 (2008): 19-32.
Recidivism after residential treatment for a sex offence was studied for 114 male adolescent juvenile sex offenders. The juveniles had been treated for an average period of two years and four months. The median time at risk after leaving the institution was nine years. Almost a third of the young men re-offended with a serious offence. Eleven % committed a sex offence; 27% committed a non-sexual violent offence; approximately a third of the respondents re-offended with a range of other acts; and 30% did not re-offend at all. Sexual recidivism appears to be related to the prior selection of a (very) young victim, and choice as a victim of a girl from outside the offender's family. Seventy % of sexual recidivism takes place during the first three years after discharge. Violent recidivism is linked with the offender's ethnicity, parental neglect, the quality of relationships with peers and classification by the institution as an opportunistic sex offender. We recommend greater differentiation in treatment offered, and improvement of follow-up provision. [ABSTRACT FROM AUTHOR]

Kimonis, Eva R., Amanda Fanniff, Randy Borum, and Kevin Elliott. “Clinician’s Perceptions of Indicators of Amenability to Sex Offender-Specific Treatment in Juveniles.” *Sexual Abuse: A Journal of Research & Treatment* 23, no. 2 (2011): 193-211.
Identifying and understanding the factors that predict treatment success is central to legal and clinical decision making about juveniles who commit sexual offenses. The current study surveyed 158 treatment providers who work with juvenile sexual offenders to explore empirically the construct of amenability as it relates to juvenile sex offender—specific treatment

(SOST). Youths' unwillingness to alter deviant sexual interest/attitudes and unsupportive parenting were rated as strong indicators of poor SOST amenability, whereas the youths' motivation for change and belief in the efficacy of treatment, strong social support and positive attachments, and resilient personality traits were rated as strong indicators of good SOST amenability. Items distinctly rated as indicators of either poor or good treatment amenability (N = 48) were thematically grouped into internally consistent scales (α's ranging from .75-.87) reflecting several possible dimensions of amenability. [ABSTRACT FROM PUBLISHER]

Letourneau, Elizabeth J., Dipankar Bandyopadhyay, Kevin S. Armstrong, and Debajyoti Sinha. "Do Sex Offender Registration and Notification Requirements Deter Juvenile Sex Crimes?" *Criminal Justice & Behavior* 37, no. 5 (2010): 553-569.

This study examined whether South Carolina's sex offender registration and notification (SORN) policy was associated with a general deterrent effect on juvenile sex crimes. Using juvenile justice data from 1991 through 2004, trend analyses modeled the intervention effects of 1995 (the year South Carolina's SORN policy was initially implemented) and 1999 (the year the policy was revised to include online registration). Initial results suggested a significant deterrent effect of SORN on first-time juvenile sex crimes. However, comparison analyses with nonsex offenses identified a similar effect on first-time robbery crimes. Follow-up analyses indicated that the apparent declines identified for first-time sex and robbery offenses were due to another legislative change, also enacted in 1995, that moved the prosecution of 16-year-old defendants from juvenile to adult court. When these cases were included in the database, follow-up analyses indicated no significant effect for the 1995 intervention year. Thus, South Carolina's SORN policy was not associated with a general deterrent effect on juvenile sex crimes. Specific policy changes are suggested regarding the application of registration and notification requirements to juveniles.

Ogloff, James R.P., Margaret C. Cutajar, Emily Mann, and Paul Mullen. *Child Sexual Abuse and Subsequent Offending and Victimization: A 45 Year Follow-Up Study*. Canberra: Australian Institute of Criminology, 2012.

The impact of sexual abuse as a child on that individual's later offending or re-victimization as an adult is examined. Sections of this report cover: subsequent offending by childhood sexual abuse (CSA) victims;

subsequent victimization of CSA victims; association between CSA and offending; association between CSA and victimization; and mediating factors between CSA and offending. Victims of childhood sexual assault "were almost five times more likely than the general population to be charged with any offence than their non-abused counterparts, with strongest associations found for sexual and violent offences. CSA victims were also more likely to have been victims of crime, particularly crimes of a sexual or violent nature. This research highlights the need for therapeutic interventions targeted at adolescent male CSA victims, particularly with regard to offender treatment programs, where many programs currently do not allow for exploration of offenders' own sexual victimization" (p. 1). http://www.aic.gov.au/publications/current%20series/tandi/421-440/tandi440.aspx http://nicic.gov/Library/026183

Pittman, Nicole, and Quyen Nguyen. A Snapshot of Juvenile Sex Offender Registration and Notification Laws: A Survey of the United States. Washington, DC: National Juvenile Justice Network, 2011.

"In light of the mottled condition of sex offender registration and notification laws across the country, and the fact that this book was started less than a year before the final deadline for states to come into compliance with SORNA, our goal is to provide a straightforward reference guide during this time of great flux" (p. 1). One can use this survey to see how different states compare to each other in regards to the Adam Walsh Act. This publication is divided into seven parts: introduction; the Adam Walsh Act—Sex Offender Registration and Notification Act (SORNA); individual state registration and notification requirements applied to children; comprehensive chart of SORNA applied to children in the states; individual fact sheets on SORNA applied to children; and Directory of State Sex Offender Registration Administrators. http://www.njjn.org/article/report-juvenile-sex-offender-laws-inconsistent

Righthand, Sue; Nina Boulard, Julia Cabral, Asia Serwik. "Reducing Sexual Offending Among Juveniles in Maine: A Systems Approach." *Corrections Today* 73, no. 1 (2011): 24-27.

The article discusses an integrated approach used by the Division of Juvenile Services (DJS) of the Maine Department of Corrections to reduce the commission of sex offenses by juveniles. Statistics on juvenile sex crimes are noted and differences between juvenile and adult sex offenders are discussed. Aspects of Maine's system including its goals and objectives, assessment protocols used, and funding received for the program's expansion are discussed.

Van Vugt, Eveline, Jessica Asscher, Jan Hendriks, Geert Jan Stams, Catrien Bijleveld, and Peter van der Laan. "Assessment of Moral Judgment and Empathy in Young Sex Offenders: A Comparison of Clinical Judgment and Test Results." *International Journal of Offender Therapy & Comparative Criminology* 56, no. 7 (2012): 986-996.

Professional decision making in forensic clinical practice may have lifelong consequences for offenders. Although information on moral development is important for prediction of reoffending and referral to adequate treatment, conclusions regarding moral development are still largely based on unstructured clinical judgment instead of assessment instruments. For this study, the authors examined to what extent unstructured clinical judgment of both moral judgment and victim empathy concurred with test results in a group of young sex offenders. Moral judgment was measured with the Sociomoral Reflection Measure–Short Form (SRM-SF), whereas victim empathy was measured with an extended version of the Basic Empathy Scale (BES). No significant associations were found between clinical judgment of moral judgment and the mean scores on the SRM-SF. However, clinical judgment of victim empathy was significantly associated with victim empathy on the Victim Empathy Scale but not consistently in the expected direction. Juvenile sex offenders, who were judged by clinicians to show little victim empathy, displayed lower mean scores on the Victim Empathy Scale than juvenile sex offenders who were evaluated to lack victim empathy or to have intact victim empathy. This study showed unstructured clinical judgment of moral development not to concur with test results. To improve decision-making processes regarding moral development, clinicians are advised to rely on instruments that assess moral development to inform clinical judgment. Further research is needed to examine which predictions are more accurate and to establish the predictive validity of moral development evaluations.

Van Vugt, Eveline, Geert Jan Stams, Maja Dekovic, Daan Brugman, Esther Rutten, and Jan Hendriks. "Moral Development of Solo Juvenile Sex Offenders." *Journal of Sexual Aggression* 14, no. 2 (July 2008): 99-109.

This study compared the moral development of solo juvenile male sex offenders (n = 20) and juvenile male non-offenders (n = 76), aged 13-19 years, from lower socioeconomic and educational backgrounds. The Moral Orientation Measure (MOM) was used to assess punishment- and victim-based moral orientation in sexual and non-sexual situations. Moral judgement was assessed with the Sociomoral Reflection Measure - Short Form (SRM-SF), with questions added on sexual offending and the offender's own victim(s). Offenders did not differ from non-offenders in victim-based orientation, but they showed weaker punishment-based orientation in sexual and non-sexual situations. No differences in moral judgement were found. However, lower stages of moral judgement were observed when the offenders' own victim was involved, confirming specific moral deficits in solo juvenile sex offenders. Delay in moral judgement proved to be associated with cognitive distortions. It was concluded that the treatment of solo juvenile sex offenders should challenge own victim-related cognitive distortions. [ABSTRACT FROM AUTHOR];

Wanklyn, Sonya G., Ashley K. Ward, Nicole S. Cormier, David M. Day, and Jennifer E. Newman. "Can We Distinguish Juvenile Violent Sex Offenders, Violent Non-sex Offenders, and Versatile Violent Sex Offenders Based on Childhood Risk Factors?" *Journal of Interpersonal Violence* 27, no. 11 (Oct 2012): 2128-2143.

Understanding the developmental precursors of juvenile violent sex offending can contribute to the promotion of effective early intervention and prevention programs for high-risk children and youth. However, there is currently a lack of research on the early characteristics of adolescents who commit violent sex offenses. Drawing on the literature regarding the generalist and specialist positions of criminal behavior, the aim of the present study was to compare childhood risk factors for three groups of juvenile offenders: (a) pure sex offenders (PSO; n = 28); (b) violent non-sex offenders (VNSO; n = 172); and (c) versatile violent sex offenders (VVSO; n = 24). Nineteen risk factors comprising four life domains (individual, family, peer, and school) were identified from a file review. Three hierarchical logistic regression analyses examined associations between risk factors and offender groups. The results reflected the underlying heterogeneity of the sample, offering support for both the specialist and generalist positions of criminal behavior. PSOs differed from VNSOs on the basis of higher odds for precocious sexual behavior. Second, VVSOs differed from VNSOs on the basis of higher odds for precocious sexual behavior, criminal family members, and an adolescent mother, as well as lower odds for poor school behavior. Third, PSOs were marginally more likely to have engaged in early overt antisocial behavior compared with VVSOs. Fourth, many of the childhood risk factors examined were not associated with any offender group. In conclusion, VVSOs appeared to differ on the greatest number of risk factors from VNSOs, suggesting that VVSOs share a more similar developmental pathway with PSOs. The prevention and future research implications of these findings are discussed. [ABSTRACT FROM PUBLISHER];

Zimring, Franklin E., Alex R. Piquero, and Wesley G. Jennings. "Sexual Delinquency in Racine: Does Early Sex Offending Predict Later Sex Offending in Youth and Young Adulthood?" *Criminology & Public Policy* 6, no. 3 (2007): 507-534.

One recent aspect of discourse about sex offenders is a debate about whether juvenile sex offending should be targeted with adult–style registration and stigma. But data on sex offending are quite thin, and data on the link between juvenile sex offending and adult careers are almost

INDEX

#

21st century, 106

A

abuse, 36, 45, 94, 102, 114, 133, 138
academic performance, 59
access, 36, 45, 78, 81, 83, 97, 104, 118
accountability, viii, 2, 3, 10, 20, 21, 23, 24, 36, 37, 80, 127, 132
ACF, 91
actuarial risk assessment, 69
Adam Walsh Act, 141
Administration for Children and Families, 91
administrators, 96, 120, 122, 132, 134
adolescent behavior, 70, 110
adolescent development, 48, 79, 99, 125, 129
adolescent sex offenders, 113
adolescents, 57, 66, 68, 69, 73, 87, 115, 120, 134, 143
adult convictions, 114
adulthood, 55, 93, 104, 121
adults, viii, 2, 3, 5, 6, 7, 15, 24, 31, 33, 37, 38, 46, 47, 62, 69, 73, 78, 81, 97, 99, 101, 109, 113, 114, 118, 120, 133, 134
advancement, 81, 132
advocacy, 22, 34
African-American, 47, 65
age, 5, 6, 12, 17, 22, 31, 33, 45, 46, 49, 50, 51, 52, 55, 59, 61, 69, 71, 75, 81, 82, 86, 95, 99, 101, 106, 114, 126, 134, 136, 137, 139
agencies, vii, 3, 6, 8, 10, 11, 13, 16, 20, 26, 27, 28, 29, 30, 31, 34, 35, 36, 37, 38, 40, 54, 56, 60, 63, 73, 74, 75, 80, 87, 91, 95, 104, 108, 120, 121, 124, 129, 133
aggressive behavior, 116
alcohol abuse, 16
alcohol consumption, 54
alcohol problems, 83
alcohol use, 135
alienation, 127
American Bar Association, 113, 117
American Samoa, 12, 33, 41, 42
anger, 109, 127
annotation, vii, viii
antisocial behavior, 62, 87, 143
anxiety, 90
anxiety disorder, 90
appropriations, 2, 12, 17, 18, 19, 20, 25, 41
Appropriations Act, 19
arrest, 51, 53, 55, 77, 83, 86, 88, 105, 127
arrests, 4, 46, 85
arson, 56
Asia, 141
assault, 36, 41, 51, 57, 59, 103, 105, 138, 140

assessment, vii, viii, 53, 55, 56, 58, 60, 61, 62, 63, 64, 65, 66, 67, 68, 69, 70, 71, 73, 74, 75, 77, 78, 83, 84, 87, 88, 95, 99, 102, 109, 111, 119, 120, 123, 137, 141, 142
assessment tools, vii, viii, 69, 74, 75
assets, 60, 68, 84, 103, 106, 128
attitudes, 89, 95, 108, 126, 139
Attorney General, viii, 2, 6, 7, 10, 11, 20, 21, 22, 29, 32, 34, 62
attribution, 107
attribution theory, 107
authority, 4, 6, 10, 13, 29, 32, 33
awareness, 56, 114

B

background information, vii, 3
ban, 50
barriers, 78, 93, 101, 122
base, 39, 69, 105, 138
base rate(s), 69
behavior of children, 79
behavior therapy, 121
behaviors, 115, 116, 124
benchmarks, 24, 119
benefits, 61, 73, 75
bias, 36
bipolar disorder, 45
brain, 100, 101, 110
budget deficit, 101
bullying, 60, 139
Bureau of Indian Affairs, 33

C

caregivers, 83
case law, 98, 107
case studies, 68, 88, 103, 128
case study, 124
CDC, 47
certification, 85
challenges, 60, 61, 63, 79, 90, 93, 96, 98, 101, 112, 115, 117, 120, 122, 123, 138
checks and balances, 81
Chicago, 5, 6, 39, 63, 74, 97, 113
child abuse, 14, 16, 27, 35, 36, 41, 138
child protective services, 38
childhood, 49, 54, 115, 140, 143
childhood sexual abuse, 140
children, 5, 6, 7, 8, 11, 48, 49, 50, 62, 71, 79, 80, 84, 93, 102, 109, 115, 121, 129, 130, 132, 133, 134, 138, 141, 143
chimera, 90
cities, 8, 58, 92
citizens, 6, 132
City, 40, 87, 102, 103
classification, 72, 86, 128, 139
climate, 78
clinical judgment, 142
clothing, 128
clusters, 96
coercion, 96
collaboration, 46, 90, 97, 109
collaborative approaches, 138
collateral, 101
College Station, 58
color, 79, 101
Commonwealth of the Northern Mariana Islands, 12, 33
communication, 84
communities, 16, 27, 55, 62, 63, 64, 86, 90, 96, 98, 107, 111, 114, 125, 127, 132, 133
community relations, 104
community service, 6, 36, 37, 74
community-based services, 50, 73, 80, 99, 126
compensation, 30
complement, 130
compliance, 15, 19, 33, 35, 37, 38, 84, 141
composition, 35, 106
conception, viii, 2
conduct disorder, 56
conference, 7
confidentiality, 4, 99, 128
confinement, 34, 35, 38, 49, 65, 80, 92, 97, 120, 126, 127
conflict, 57

Congress, viii, 1, 2, 3, 4, 6, 7, 8, 9, 11, 19, 23, 24, 25, 26, 27, 28, 29, 32, 34, 40, 41
consensus, 8, 9, 47, 48, 75, 80, 119
consent, 59
consolidation, 16
conviction, 53, 55, 59, 77, 101
cooperation, 108
coordination, 3, 12, 14, 18, 27, 28, 33, 78
correlation(s), 41, 65, 73
cost, 55, 61, 79, 83, 90, 93, 97, 99, 100, 101, 102, 120, 121, 123, 126, 129
cost saving, 79, 101
cost-benefit analysis, 61, 83, 129
counsel, 8, 99, 129
counseling, 14, 26, 36, 37, 39
covering, 59, 129
crimes, vii, viii, 1, 2, 3, 4, 16, 17, 20, 22, 31, 32, 33, 41, 50, 79, 85, 95, 101, 102, 111, 113, 114, 135, 140, 141
criminal activity, 92, 95, 138
criminal behavior, 59, 87, 143
criminal gangs, 17
criminal justice system, 5, 6, 31, 48, 49, 50, 55, 61, 78, 85, 90, 106, 114, 120, 123, 130
criminal system, 4, 114
CSA, 140
CST, 50
culture, 78, 79, 95, 122

D

data collection, 103, 115
data set, 98, 111
database, 131, 132, 140
decision makers, 83, 97
decision-making process, 142
defendants, 6, 50, 140
deficit, 90
deinstitutionalization, 31
delinquency, 4, 6, 7, 12, 14, 18, 19, 25, 29, 30, 31, 37, 39, 45, 48, 49, 50, 51, 52, 53, 54, 56, 68, 94, 97, 100, 101, 105, 115, 116, 129, 130, 131, 132, 133, 135
delinquent behavior, 27, 32, 93, 96, 117
demographic characteristics, 57, 85
Department of Agriculture, 27
Department of Education, 27, 93, 122
Department of Health and Human Services, 27
Department of Justice, 4, 9, 16, 17, 18, 19, 28, 38, 39, 40, 41, 49, 51, 57, 83, 98
Department of Labor, 27
depression, 115
depth, 103, 124, 127
detainees, 54, 109, 112
detention, 6, 11, 14, 15, 20, 23, 24, 31, 33, 34, 36, 38, 46, 48, 49, 51, 52, 60, 63, 66, 71, 77, 79, 82, 84, 90, 91, 93, 96, 99, 102, 107, 112, 114, 118, 120, 121, 122, 123, 127, 129, 131
developmental psychology, 90
dignity, 133
disability, 93, 106
disclosure, 57
discrimination, 60, 128
disposition, 50, 52, 77, 85, 136
distortions, 143
distribution, 17
District of Columbia, 23, 41, 80, 119, 126, 128
DOJ, 4, 8, 10, 19, 27, 29, 32, 33
dominance, 9
dose-response relationship, 92
downsizing, 80, 126
drawing, 126
drug abuse, 14, 26
drug offense, 77
drugs, 37, 54, 103
due process, 6, 49, 63, 99
dynamic factors, 68, 71
dynamic risk factors, 75

E

economics, 127
education, 8, 16, 22, 26, 34, 36, 37, 40, 60, 69, 71, 78, 82, 86, 93, 94, 98, 102, 114, 118, 121, 124, 128, 132, 133
educational assessment, 63, 124

educational background, 142
educational programs, 18, 39, 86, 93, 121, 125
educational services, 86
educational settings, 112
emotional disorder, 95
emotional health, 112, 117, 127
empathy, 142
employees, 11, 25, 35, 44, 128
employment, 34, 101
empowerment, 68, 103, 128
encouragement, 68, 103, 128
enforcement, 22, 57
enrollment, 101
environment, 14, 87, 128
environmental factors, 56
ethnic groups, 133
ethnicity, 52, 53, 67, 72, 106, 139
evidence, 18, 21, 25, 27, 45, 55, 56, 71, 75, 83, 87, 88, 91, 92, 94, 99, 105, 108, 110, 115, 123, 125, 129, 132, 133, 135, 136
evidence-based program, 88, 92, 99, 115, 129, 132
evolution, vii, 3
exclusion, 79
exercise, 10, 29
expenditures, 14, 22, 97
exploitation, 59
exposure, 135

F

fairness, 126
faith, 107
families, 5, 14, 16, 19, 27, 34, 80, 96, 108, 126, 127, 130, 133
family functioning, 87
family members, 104, 138, 143
family relationships, 89
family support, 71
family violence, 138
fear, 109
federal agency, 4, 11, 28
Federal Emergency Management Agency, 56
federal government, vii, viii, 1, 2, 4, 6, 7, 8, 9, 10, 11, 19, 20, 24, 27, 28, 29, 30
Federal Government, 7, 28
federal law, 6, 7, 93, 98, 121, 133
feelings, 127
FEMA, 56
fidelity, 78, 87
financial, 4, 81, 82
financial incentives, 82
flexibility, 21, 41
formula, 3, 12, 13, 14, 16, 22, 31, 32, 33, 34, 35, 36, 38, 40
foundations, 105
funding, viii, 2, 3, 4, 5, 8, 9, 12, 13, 14, 17, 19, 20, 21, 22, 23, 24, 25, 26, 27, 28, 31, 32, 33, 34, 35, 36, 37, 38, 39, 40, 41, 42, 45, 97, 141
funds, 4, 8, 11, 12, 13, 14, 17, 22, 25, 31, 80, 126

G

gangs, 20, 35, 36, 37, 57
gender differences, 70
generalizability, 75
Georgia, 98, 125, 132
government expenditure, 22
governments, 4, 17, 21, 22
grades, 46
grant programs, vii, viii, 1, 2, 3, 4, 9, 10, 16, 17, 18, 19, 23, 24, 25, 26, 28, 30, 34, 35, 38, 39, 50
grants, viii, 2, 3, 7, 8, 10, 13, 16, 17, 18, 19, 20, 21, 22, 31, 34, 35, 36, 37, 38, 42
group treatment, 96
growth, 4, 55, 124, 137
guidance, 50, 123
guidelines, 83, 89, 122, 123, 124
guiding principles, 75
guilty, 114

H

harassment, 60, 128

Hawaii, 98
health, 18, 46, 49, 50, 57, 60, 73, 82, 90, 94, 99, 115, 117
Health and Human Services, 11, 90
health care, 57, 82
health problems, 73
health risks, 115
heterogeneity, 73, 143
hiring, 20, 94
historical overview, 106
history, 48, 53, 54, 71, 81, 108, 112, 114, 134
homelessness, 101
homes, 60, 87, 122
homicide, 50, 85
House, 8, 11, 35, 40
housing, 47, 90, 120, 129
Housing and Urban Development, 11, 29
human, 48, 78
human right(s), 48

I

ID, 95
ideal(s), 63, 79, 123
identification, 71, 75, 110, 137
identity, 122
Immigration and Customs Enforcement, 11
immunity, 44
imprisonment, 95
improvements, 78, 89
incarceration, 14, 50, 81, 87, 91, 99, 100, 118, 123, 130
income, 16
independence, 32, 84
individual character, 80
individual characteristics, 80
individuals, 30, 31, 33, 35, 38, 40, 47, 57, 86, 93, 102, 109, 113, 121, 125, 130, 133, 138
Individuals with Disabilities Education Improvement Act, 122
industry, 132
ineffectiveness, 24, 71
inefficiency, 8
inequality, 79, 117
information sharing, 20
injury, 57
inmates, 15, 57
institutions, viii, 1, 5, 9, 28, 31, 34, 36, 45, 54, 99, 107, 109, 122
integration, 79, 129
integrity, 111
internal consistency, 136
internalizing, 115
interpersonal skills, 94
intersex, 124, 128
intervention, 18, 35, 47, 65, 74, 84, 87, 89, 90, 91, 95, 99, 100, 112, 122, 129, 131, 132, 137, 140, 143
investment, 25, 80, 126
isolation, 114, 120, 127, 138
issues, 2, 3, 13, 21, 23, 24, 27, 36, 42, 50, 56, 57, 58, 75, 76, 77, 90, 97, 98, 99, 110, 114, 117, 123, 124, 129, 131, 132, 137

J

JABG, viii, 2, 19, 20, 21, 22, 23, 24, 41
JJDPA, vii, viii, 1, 2, 3, 4, 5, 9, 10, 12, 13, 14, 16, 17, 18, 19, 23, 24, 25, 26, 28, 29, 30, 31, 32, 33, 34, 35, 36, 37, 38, 39, 40, 41, 45
job skills, 37
Jordan, 119
Judicial Branch, 93, 121
jurisdiction, 13, 21, 22, 33, 40, 44, 51, 52, 61, 77, 88, 99, 101, 108
just society, 133
Juvenile Accountability Block Grant, viii, 2, 19
juvenile court systems, vii, 1, 4, 107
juvenile crime, 2, 4, 8, 23, 44, 51, 65, 105, 106
juvenile delinquency, viii, 2, 4, 7, 8, 9, 10, 11, 12, 13, 14, 15, 16, 17, 18, 19, 27, 28, 29, 30, 31, 33, 34, 39, 40, 41, 86, 96
juvenile delinquents, 7, 91, 103, 116
juvenile detention facilities, 50, 60, 82

juvenile drug courts, 20
juvenile justice agencies, vii, 3, 75, 133
Juvenile Justice and Delinquency Prevention Act, vii, viii, 1, 3, 9, 28, 34, 45
juvenile justice efforts, viii, 1, 2, 9, 23, 28, 29, 33
juvenile justice systems, vii, viii, 1, 2, 3, 4, 5, 6, 7, 9, 10, 12, 15, 20, 22, 23, 24, 27, 28, 30, 31, 62, 78, 88, 96, 99, 105, 118, 127
juvenile offenders, vii, viii, 2, 4, 7, 9, 10, 14, 15, 16, 21, 23, 24, 27, 28, 30, 36, 41, 54, 55, 58, 67, 71, 82, 84, 85, 86, 87, 89, 91, 92, 95, 98, 99, 104, 106, 116, 129, 136, 143
juvenile sex offender, vii, viii, 61, 62, 104, 113, 135, 136, 138, 139, 142, 143

K

kill, 58

L

landscape, 67
language barrier, 14
language development, 110
language skills, 110
law enforcement, 8, 40, 57, 61, 71
laws, vii, 2, 4, 5, 6, 21, 23, 32, 43, 44, 48, 49, 63, 87, 99, 101, 134, 141
lead, viii, 2, 4, 10, 48, 59, 93, 103, 125
leadership, 18, 37, 45, 79, 97, 127, 130, 133
leadership development, 37, 130, 133
learning, 14, 16
learning difficulties, 16
learning disabilities, 14
legal protection, 7, 89
legislation, vii, viii, 1, 3, 4, 7, 9, 25, 44, 52, 98, 129, 131, 132, 136
leisure, 116
lens, 71, 90
lifetime, 50
light, 62, 141
literacy, 16
litigation, 37, 114
local government, viii, 2, 4, 8, 13, 18, 19, 20, 21, 22, 25, 31, 32, 37, 40
Louisiana, 74
low risk, 48

M

magnitude, 89
mainstream society, 86
majority, 5, 11, 30, 35, 40, 46, 56, 80, 87, 94
maltreatment, 41, 54
management, 30, 50, 56, 62, 63, 64, 69, 74, 80, 83, 84, 88, 119, 120, 128, 138
manslaughter, 41
marijuana, 65, 103
materials, 104, 134
media, 45, 96
median, 139
mediation, 36
Medicaid, 129
medical, 60, 94, 128
membership, 118
mental disorder, 82
mental health, 13, 14, 16, 18, 21, 25, 26, 37, 45, 50, 54, 56, 60, 64, 73, 75, 82, 83, 88, 90, 94, 95, 99, 115, 116, 117, 128, 129, 132, 138
mental health professionals, 90
mental illness, 48, 56, 106, 109
mental state, 58
mentoring, 14, 16, 26, 35, 37, 81, 131
mentoring program, 16, 37
meta-analysis, 70, 88, 105
methodology, 59, 61, 63, 68, 88, 103, 119, 128
Mexico, 67
Miami, 84, 96
migration, 57
military, 37
minorities, 15, 24
minors, 11, 59

mission, vii, 1, 3, 6, 30, 124, 129, 130, 133
Missouri, 76, 96
model system, 106
models, 56, 83, 91, 95, 116, 128
modifications, 33
modules, 50, 94
modus operandi, 137
MOM, 142
momentum, 9
mood disorder, 90
moral development, 142
moral judgment, 142
moral reasoning, 127
motivation, 71, 112, 128, 139
murder, 41, 59

N

National Survey, 45, 102
National Youth Gang Survey, 57
needy, 7, 84
neglect, 14, 16, 36, 133, 139
neuroscience, 110
New Zealand, 95
nonprofit organizations, 32, 36
non-sex offenders, 143
null, 92
nutrition, 115

O

obstacles, 93, 122
Office of Justice Programs(OJP), 40, 41, 112, 116, 130
Office of Juvenile Justice and Delinquency Prevention, vii, 3, 29, 39, 40, 41, 44, 49, 51, 57, 77, 83, 88, 98, 105, 116, 131, 134
Office of National Drug Control Policy, 11
officials, 120
OJJDP, vii, 3, 4, 10, 11, 12, 13, 15, 16, 17, 18, 19, 24, 25, 26, 27, 29, 30, 32, 33, 34, 38, 39, 40, 41, 42, 44, 47, 57, 67, 118, 131
Oklahoma, 40
operating system, 109
operations, 11, 30, 49, 61, 89, 119
opportunities, 27, 93, 115, 121, 136
overlap, 19, 26, 27, 28
oversight, 89

P

Pacific, 33, 42
parallel, 81
parental involvement, 108
parenting, 36, 139
parents, 5, 55, 84, 97, 104, 107, 108, 137
parole, 50, 63, 81, 99, 102, 115, 118
participants, 95, 96, 108, 116
pathways, 93, 114, 122
peer group, 138
peer influence, 106
peer relationship, 89
permit, 16
perseverance, 79
personality, 94, 139
personality characteristics, 94
personality traits, 139
physical health, 115
pilot study, 116
plea bargaining, 81
police, 6, 22, 57, 113
policy, 11, 25, 26, 29, 47, 48, 52, 59, 65, 81, 82, 88, 90, 92, 98, 101, 105, 107, 110, 113, 116, 117, 119, 120, 128, 129, 130, 136, 140
policy initiative, 88
policy issues, 92, 119
policy makers, 107, 120, 129
policy options, 25, 26
policymakers, 58, 101, 119
population, 4, 12, 17, 22, 24, 27, 46, 54, 63, 64, 66, 85, 93, 101, 107, 114, 118, 119, 121, 123, 124, 134, 135, 138, 140
positive mood, 112
positive reinforcement, 84
poverty, 16, 94, 106, 117
predictive accuracy, 61, 75

predictive validity, 53, 54, 58, 62, 65, 66, 70, 75, 136, 142
pregnancy, 115, 118
preparation, 30
president, 11, 30, 35
prevalence rate, 57
prevention, 4, 7, 10, 14, 15, 17, 18, 19, 25, 26, 27, 29, 30, 31, 32, 34, 35, 37, 39, 61, 99, 129, 131, 132, 143
principles, 64, 75, 102, 104, 116, 119
prisons, 47, 81, 90, 114, 118, 127
private sector, 18, 30
probation officers, 5, 16, 20, 26, 39, 69, 94, 108
problem behavior, 103
procedural rule, 5
professional development, 94
professionals, 7, 83, 90, 109, 121, 123, 132
profit, 130
program administration, 9, 128
program outcomes, 88, 111
program staff, 86
programming, 85, 86, 89, 93, 98, 99, 111, 117, 120, 121
project, 47, 59, 71
proportionality, 50, 126
proposition, 6, 95
protection, 5, 8, 49, 71, 114
protective factors, 71, 72, 112
psychologist, 60
psychometric properties, 136
psychopaths, 72
psychopathy, 72
psychosocial functioning, 83, 116
public awareness, 8, 60
public concern, 86
public opinion, 101
public policy, 110, 113, 133
public resources, 63
public safety, 21, 41, 80, 81, 92, 97, 100, 102, 112, 114, 115, 123, 126, 130, 132
public schools, 122
Puerto Rico, 41, 130
punishment, viii, 1, 4, 5, 7, 24, 50, 108, 142

Q

quality of service, 132
questioning, 113, 128
questionnaire, 103
quotas, 15, 25, 38

R

race, 45, 46, 51, 52, 53, 65, 79, 94, 106, 108, 112, 129
rape, 41
reactions, 105
recall, 99
recidivism, 47, 48, 53, 54, 55, 58, 59, 61, 62, 65, 66, 67, 69, 70, 74, 75, 78, 79, 81, 83, 84, 86, 89, 91, 93, 96, 99, 100, 103, 108, 111, 121, 132, 135, 139
recidivism rate, 91, 103
recommendations, 11, 30, 48, 50, 63, 66, 71, 72, 78, 81, 85, 88, 94, 96, 101, 102, 103, 105, 109, 114, 117, 118, 119, 120, 124, 126
reconciliation, 34
recreation, 37
recreational, 18, 116
reform(s), 7, 43, 44, 55, 62, 65, 68, 79, 81, 85, 87, 96, 97, 99, 101, 102, 103, 104, 105, 117, 118, 119, 120, 121, 123, 125, 126, 127, 128, 129, 130, 133
registration laws, 135
regression, 46, 66, 85, 86, 138, 143
regression analysis, 46, 86, 138
regulations, 33
rehabilitation, viii, 1, 2, 3, 4, 7, 10, 23, 24, 27, 29, 32, 50, 55, 66, 80, 85, 90, 97, 100, 102, 107, 118, 126
reimburse, 30
relevance, 68
reliability, 67, 68, 136
relief, 84
remediation, 50
remorse, 100
replication, 56

reproduction, 115
requirements, 12, 13, 14, 19, 22, 25, 33, 34, 140, 141
researchers, 113, 129, 132
Residential, 76, 96, 121, 122, 139
resilience, 91
resistance, 128
resolution, 81
resources, vii, viii, 20, 26, 32, 45, 59, 60, 74, 79, 81, 91, 92, 99, 111, 129, 130, 133, 134, 135, 138
response, 2, 4, 23, 27, 51, 82, 84, 97, 105, 107, 111, 122, 124
restitution, 34, 36
restrictions, 13, 31, 61
rewards, 80, 126
rights, 49, 63, 78, 114, 118, 120
risk assessment, 56, 58, 61, 62, 65, 69, 70, 71, 72, 73, 74, 75, 117, 129
risk factors, 54, 58, 68, 71, 72, 75, 87, 93, 112, 115, 116, 143
risk management, 71
risks, 47, 66, 72, 84, 93, 137
RNA, 69
routes, 139
rowing, 60
rules, 44, 134
rural areas, 13, 14

S

safety, 21, 56, 57, 76, 93, 96, 104, 107, 109, 112, 115, 121
sanctions, viii, 2, 10, 20, 21, 24, 32, 36, 41, 49, 84, 92, 96, 132
savings, 101
scholarship, 16
school, 14, 16, 20, 21, 26, 32, 34, 36, 46, 58, 78, 86, 93, 97, 98, 101, 103, 111, 112, 117, 121, 123, 127, 143
school failure, 118
science, 110, 118
scope, 19, 33
secondary data, 80
secondary schools, 58
security, 107, 124
self-esteem, 112, 138
self-identity, 128
self-report data, 55
self-sufficiency, 91, 115
Senate, 11, 35, 99
sentencing, 5, 32, 50, 63, 81, 85, 99, 101
service provider, 71
services, 13, 14, 16, 18, 19, 21, 26, 27, 28, 31, 34, 36, 37, 41, 46, 47, 57, 79, 80, 82, 83, 84, 85, 86, 87, 89, 90, 92, 93, 94, 95, 98, 105, 107, 113, 116, 117, 121, 122, 125, 126, 130, 132, 134, 137
sex, 45, 54, 59, 62, 86, 101, 113, 135, 136, 137, 139, 140, 141, 142, 143, 144
sex offenders, 62, 113, 135, 136, 138, 139, 141, 142, 143, 144
sexual abuse, 122, 140
sexual behavior, 112, 117, 136, 143
sexual offences, 138
sexual offending, 113, 135, 142
sexual orientation, 129
sexual recidivism, 61, 69, 136, 139
sexual violence, 135
sexuality, 115
shape, viii, 2, 90
shareholders, 61
shock, 87
showing, 50
SII, 62
skills training, 18
social problems, 122, 130
social responsibility, 37
social skills, 89, 115, 127
social skills training, 127
social structure, 69
social support, 84, 112, 139
social support network, 84
society, 24, 47, 86, 93, 121, 125, 130
solution, 45, 92, 109, 127, 130
special education, 93, 94, 98, 121
specialists, 113, 132
specific knowledge, 95
staff development, 119, 132
staff members, 122

State Formula Grants Program, vii, 3, 12
states, vii, viii, 1, 2, 3, 4, 5, 6, 7, 8, 9, 10, 12, 13, 14, 17, 18, 20, 21, 22, 23, 24, 25, 27, 28, 30, 31, 32, 33, 34, 35, 37, 38, 40, 41, 44, 49, 50, 80, 82, 91, 97, 105, 109, 111, 119, 123, 126, 130, 133, 141
statistics, 30, 47, 48, 65
statutes, 50
stigma, 144
stigmatized, 122
structural changes, 65
structural modifications, 82
structure, 17, 25, 62, 74, 94, 103
structuring, 108
style, 37, 144
subgroups, 53, 72, 137
subsidy, 7, 18
substance abuse, 18, 21, 25, 36, 37, 45, 54, 59, 84, 94, 99, 116, 118, 132
substance use, 71, 83, 90, 99, 115, 116
success rate, 87
suicide, 54
supervision, 5, 6, 36, 37, 65, 66, 74, 76, 77, 81, 83, 96, 99, 114
support services, 16
Supreme Court, 7, 8, 40, 50, 62
surveillance, 63, 87
sustainability, 82, 87
Switzerland, 134

T

target, 26, 80
target population, 80
Task Force, 61
teachers, 93, 122, 134
team members, 45
technical assistance, 4, 17, 34, 130
techniques, 31, 84, 112
technology, 71
teens, 57, 60, 81, 138
telecommunications, 107
tension, 23
term plans, 10
territory, 12
testing, 71, 89, 105
theft, 103
therapeutic benefits, 92
therapeutic interventions, 141
therapeutic relationship, 94
therapy, 121
time frame, 66
time periods, 69
Title I, 8, 19, 29, 35, 36, 37, 38, 39
Title II, 19, 29, 35, 36, 37, 38, 39
Title V, 18, 19, 26, 35, 37, 49
tobacco, 112, 117
tracks, 48
traffic violations, 55
training, vii, viii, 8, 10, 14, 16, 20, 26, 27, 29, 30, 36, 37, 79, 82, 86, 94, 104, 108, 122, 127, 128, 132, 134
training programs, 14, 26
trauma, 90
traumatic events, 112
traumatic experiences, 54
trial, 5, 6, 47, 49, 50, 115, 120, 136
troubleshooting, 71
tutoring, 37

U

United States, vii, 1, 3, 5, 7, 12, 17, 22, 29, 39, 40, 45, 49, 50, 56, 57, 65, 71, 102, 103, 118, 120, 132, 141
urban, 8, 15, 78, 93, 96
urban areas, 15
Urban Institute, 77
USA, 131

V

validation, 89
vandalism, 16
variables, 46, 54, 137, 138
variations, 49
victimization, 51, 105, 112, 117, 131, 140
victims, 16, 21, 27, 35, 36, 41, 61, 106, 135, 137, 140

violence, 2, 16, 20, 23, 27, 37, 41, 44, 51, 57, 66, 68, 72, 73, 105
violent behavior, 41
violent crime, 4, 12, 22, 119
violent offences, 141
violent offenders, 85
violent recidivism, 67
vision, 63, 123, 126
voluntary organizations, 30

W

waiver, 31, 51, 52
Washington, 43, 45, 47, 49, 50, 51, 53, 55, 57, 59, 60, 62, 64, 77, 78, 80, 83, 88, 89, 90, 95, 97, 98, 100, 101, 102, 104, 105, 114, 115, 116, 117, 119, 120, 124, 125, 126, 128, 129, 141
water, 20
web, 82
websites, vii, viii
welfare, 6, 7, 38, 60, 62, 106
well-being, 91
White House, 7
Wisconsin, 113
witnesses, 8
workers, 67, 80
working class, 79
wrongdoing, 130

Y

Yale University, 93, 121
young adults, 138
young delinquents, vii, 1, 3
young people, 60, 64, 66, 97, 100, 101, 106, 110, 120, 122, 138
young women, vii, viii, 117